TURNED CHESSMEN

FOR COLLECTORS, PLAYERS AND WOODWORKERS

MIKE DARLOW

STOBART DAVIES

AMMANFORD, CARMARTHENSHIRE

Turned Chessmen is the fifth book in Mike Darlow's woodturning series published in Great Britain by Stobart Davies Limited. The first four books in the series are The Fundamentals of Woodturning, Woodturning Methods, Woodturning Techniques, and Woodturning Design.

The fonts used are Novarese and Helvetica, both set 11/13.

Printed in China by Hing Yip Printing Company Limited.

British Library Cataloguing-in-Publication Data

A catalogue record for this book is available from the British Library

ISBN 0-85442-115-7

Stobart Davies Limited,
Stobart House, Pontyclerc, Penybanc Road, Ammanford, Carmarthenshire SA18 3HP, Wales.

Tel: 01269 593100   Fax: 01269 596116   Email: sales@stobartdavies.com   www.stobartdavies.com

CONTENTS

ACKNOWLEDGEMENTS

I thank the people, companies, and organizations listed below for their advice and information; the supply of transparencies, photographs and scans; and for allowing me to photograph their work or items in their possession. Their contributions have been essential to the completion of this book.

Australia
Debra Burton, Mr and Mrs John Carroll, Adrian Hunt, Andrew Lake, Mr and Mrs Brian Lemin, Ernie Newman, John Powell, Ken Raffe.
David McLaren, Bungendore Wood Works Gallery; Carba-Tec Pty Ltd; Peter Parr, Chess Discount Sales; Neil J. Ellis, 'u Beaut Polishes.

Czech Republic
Veronika Hornerova, Lobkowicz Collections, Nelahozeves Castle.

England
Reg Hawthorn, Michael Mark.
Sylvia Crawley, Curator of the Pinto Collection, Birmingham Museums and Art Gallery; Garrick Coleman; Nick Davidson, Craft Supplies; Christopher Jaques, John Jaques & Son Limited; Oxford University Press; Robin Easton and Pam Carter, Simpson's-in-the-Strand and The Savoy Group.

France
Bibliothèque nationale de France.

Germany
Gottfried Böckelmann. Verlag Th. Schäfer.

United States of America
Steven Addams, Michael Brolly, Michael Cullen, Bonnie Klein, Bernard Lewis, Jon Sauer.
Dover Publications, Inc.; Jessie McNab, Metropolitan Museum of Art; Kevin Clay, Oneway Manufacturing; Donna Corbin, Philadelphia Museum of Art; Colleen Schafroth, Maryhill Museum of Art.

Those who have made a special contribution include

The helpful staff at my local Moss Vale and Bowral branches of the Wingecarribee Shire Library.

Des Cowley and Pam Pryde at the State Library of Victoria helped me to obtain illustrations from its Anderson Chess Collection. This collection is based on the gift to the Library by Mr Magnus Victor Anderson (1884–1966), a Melbourne accountant and a keen chess player. It now has about 12,000 items, and is recognised as one of the three largest public collections of chess literature. (The other two are the J. G. White Collection in the Cleveland Public Library, and the van der Linde-Niemeijer Collection in the Royal Library, The Hague).

I contacted Stephen Zietz at the John G. White Chess and Checkers Collection in Cleveland Public Library for details of the Copley counters which I had seen mentioned in Daniel M. Liddell's *Chess Men*. Not having a copy of Copley's pamphlet, Stephen searched, located the only original in the Library of Congress, and kindly provided a copy for this book.

After hearing from Donna Corbin that I was writing this book, Doug Polumbaum generously offered images of any of the sets in his collection. His wife, Risa Korris, then took the photographs. I did not have access to a collection of chess sets to photograph, so that the offer was invaluable.

Vel and Gareth Williams have assisted by sending copies of *The Chess Collector*, and by clarifying points of which I was unsure. Gareth's splendidly illustrated book *Master Pieces* was also my main source for illustrations of chessmen which I could replicate. I then photographed my copies for *Turned Chessman*.

I am a self-publisher in rural Australia, and am only able to continue to publish this woodturning series because of the international sales. Over the past five years I have developed an excellent working relationship with Brian Davies, and more recently with Jane and Nigel Evans, of Stobart Davies in England; and Alan Giagnocavo, Peg Couch, Shannon Flowers, and more recently Mark Vogel at Fox Chapel in America.

My greatest thanks go to my wife Aliki who has has become a demon editor and proofreader, and has allowed me to sometimes reschedule some of the evergrowing list of household projects for which I am told I am responsible. Our elder son Joshua has left home leaving Samuel to cope uncomplainingly with the travails of a father who is also an author.

INTRODUCTION

This book will appeal to three distinct readerships: to woodworkers, especially woodturners, to chess-set collectors, and to chess players. However, when I started writing *Turned Chessmen*, I envisaged a short book just for woodturners, but as I progressed, I saw that those who intended to design and make chessmen would benefit greatly by gaining a knowledge of the history of chess and chessmen. I also found that designers of chess sets had contributed little to the written histories and studies of chessmen, and that woodturners had barely contributed at all. I therefore decided to describe and discuss the history, design and making of chessmen from a woodturner's and woodturning-designer's perspective, and to concentrate on turned chessmen rather than carved. *Turned Chessmen* is the result, and will, I believe, attract woodworkers to a hitherto neglected area, and provide fresh insights for chess-set collectors and chess players. Perhaps also if chess set collectors and players understand what is involved in designing and making a chess set, they may be persuaded to consider buying or commissioning chess equipment from today's craftspeople (including me).

I am a poor and only occasional chess player. Without much thought, I designed and turned a chess set in the early 1980s. In 1999 I chanced across Harry Golombek's *Chess: A History* at my local library in Bowral, and then bought *Chessmen* by A. E. J. Mackett-Beeson. Both books spurred me to design and turn three further sets. My interest in chessmen then incubated until I was free to start this book in early 2003, immediately after finishing *Woodturning Design*, the fourth book in my woodturning series. That book largely completed my writings on the basics of woodturning. My plan was then to continue the series by writing project books which would help turners exploit the basics that they had already learnt.

Turned Chessmen is the first of those project books. Its historical and design content is intended to stimulate an appreciation of chess-set designs and a desire to create new ones. But I appreciate that for many woodturners the first step into a new area of turning is to copy, and thereby gain the experience, knowledge, and confidence to then strike out alone. I have therefore provided detailed drawings in chapter 5, and practical instructions in chapter 6. These two chapters do not attempt to provide all the information you may need because I can refer you to the appropriate pages in earlier books in the series, *Woodturning Methods*, *Woodturning Techniques*, and *Woodturning Design*. The first book in the series, *The Fundamentals of Woodturning*, provides all the advice on basic woodturning techniques that you may need to supplement the making instructions in chapter 6.

This book's subjects do not include checkers (draughts), boxes for chessmen or checkers, checkered boards, or chess and games tables because they will be covered in a companion book.

Mike Darlow, August, 2004.

KEY

Center lines and axes

Hidden detail

Pointing and dimensioning

Movement

Reference lines for setting out

Fold

Make pencil mark on
revolving wood surface

Wood in elevation

Wood in section

Leading

Centers and chucks

Tool cuts

Chapter One

A HISTORY OF CHESSMEN

This chapter sketches the fascinating history of chess and particularly of turned wooden chessmen. Such knowledge is essential for the chess-set collector, invaluable for the chess-set designer, and increases the pleasure of playing chess.

In writing this chapter I have not attempted to view original sources or undertake any primary research; I have instead gleaned from the publications listed in this chapter's endnotes and in this book's bibliography. My most valuable references have been the journal *The Chess Collector*, the books *Chess: the History of a Game* by Richard Eales and *Master Pieces* by Gareth Williams, and the book to which all writings since 1913 on the histories of chess and chessmen owe much, *A History of Chess* by H. J. R. Murray.[1]

The one-and-a-half-millennia history of chessmen is incoherent without a strong leavening of conjecture because few early chessmen have survived and because of the absence of contemporary writings and illustrations earlier than the eleventh century. The inevitable and unintentional changes which occur as a design is transmitted are a further complication. Imagine turner A turns a chess set. Turner B copies it. Turner C copies turner B's set. And so on. Through incompetence, carelessness, differences in aesthetic preference, habit, and arbitrary decision, you can be sure that turner E's set would be very different to turner A's original.

TERMS

Before we set out along the path of history, I shall outline of some of the terms associated with chessmen. A chess set has thirty-two *chessmen*—they are called *men* despite two being queens and four being genderless castle towers. A chess set also has two equal *sides* called *black* and *white* irrespective of the colors of their men. Each side of sixteen men consists of the same numbers of six *pieces* (types of man). In contemporary English the six pieces are kings, queens, bishops, knights, rooks (castles), and pawns; and in the illustrations of pieces in this book they are shown in this order with the king on the left unless labelled or obviously otherwise. The

notations for the six pieces are K, Q, B, N (because the K of knight has already been taken for king), R, and P.

In each side there are one king, one queen, two bishops, two knights, two rooks, and eight pawns. Before the start of a game, each man is placed on the chess board in one, or one of several, specified positions according to its side and what piece it is. A chess board has 64 squares. The lines of squares running from right to left are called *ranks*; those running from player to player at 90° to the ranks are called *files*. During play each man has the abilities to move, take (the equivalent of kill or capture), or block opposing men in specified ways.

All men in a chess set which are the same piece are usually identical or similar in form and size. One exception is that in some sets two pawns on each side are larger. For the start of a game these larger pawns are intended to be positioned at both ends of the two ranks of pawns to maximize the attractiveness of the arrangement. If any pawn reaches the far rank during a game, it is *promoted*, usually to a queen (a side may thus contain more than one queen). One of the oversized pawns from that side is then usually substituted to represent the new queen. Other ways to represent a promoted queen are to invert a rook, apply a collar of string or ribbon to the pawn or any other captured man from that side, or substitute a coin or similar.

Chess sets can be divided into *playing* sets, and *displaying* sets. After a game you gently toss (or better place) the men of a playing set into their box. Assuming a displaying set is not too delicate or precious to play with, after a game you carefully place each of its men in its padded compartment.

1.1 INDIAN ORIGINS

The origin of chess is unknown, but it may have started in the basin of the river Ganges in northern India (figure 1.1) about A.D. 550. The first substantial Indian reference to chess is in the *Harshacharita* (Life of Harsha)—between 606 and 647 Harsha was the king of a state lying along the river Ganges. The text was written in about 625 in Sanskrit (the classical Hindu literary language based on a dialect from northwestern India). It refers to *ashtapadas* (gaming boards with sixty-four squares), and to *chaturanga* (from *chatur* meaning 'four', and *anga* meaning 'a component part or limb'). *Chaturanga* had become the Sanskrit term for chess because chess was a game of war with four of its pieces based on the four divisions of the Indian army: infantry (modern pawns), horse cavalry (knights), horse-drawn chariots (rooks), and war elephants controlled by a mahout and carrying soldiers in a howdah (bishops). The other two pieces, a shah (king), and the shah's wazir, a minister or advisor (queen), were also intimately associated with the army.

Chaturanga superficially resembled already existing games of chance which used dice or similar. Unlike them chess was and remains a game in which the moves are fully determined by human will, although arbitrariness or emotion sometimes intrude. Also, although the consensus is that most of the early variants of chess were for two players, there were variants for four players.

Chaturanga was a much more sedate game than modern chess, mainly because the wazir and war elephant were far more restricted in their movements and power than today's queen and bishop.

1.2 PERSIA

Chaturanga spread from northern India through trade and conquest. It spread north into central Asia, but made little headway to the east against the Chinese game *go* which had originated much earlier. Chaturanga also spread west into Persia late in the reign of King Khusrau (531–578), one of the native Sasanian dynasty which had ruled since A.D. 224. The Persians called chaturanga *chatrang*.

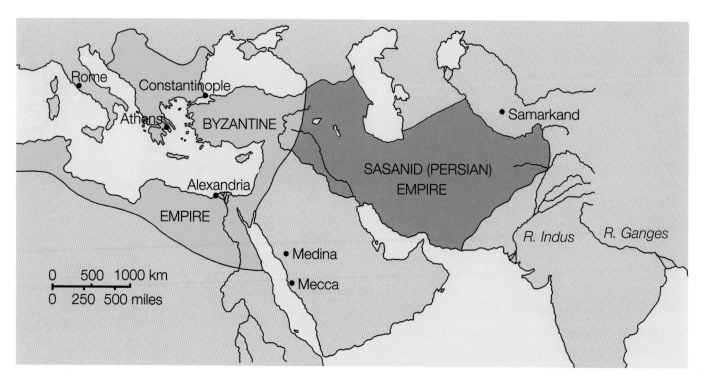

Figure 1.1 The extents of the Byzantine and Persian empires in about A.D. 650, approximately a century after chess was invented in the Ganges basin. The Byzantine empire was the eastern counterpart and successor to the western Roman Empire.

Based on the map in Bernard Lewis, *The Middle East* (London: Weidenfeld & Nicholson, 1995), page 409.

A Persian manuscript *Chatrang-namak*, written in about 635, confirms that chatrang was a game for two players, and names the six pieces used. Persian chessmen of the period were, like those used in India, figuratively carved.

1.3 ISLAM ARAB CONQUEST

Muhammad the Prophet was born in Mecca in A.D. 570 or 571. One night in about 610 the Angel Gabriel came to Muhammad and instructed him to recite a message from God. Muhammad subsequently received many more messages from God in the same way. Because Muhammad could not read or write, he later dictated these messages to scribes to create a permanent record. This record became known as the *Qur'an* (an Arabic word which combines the meanings of 'reading' and 'recitation').

Muhammad urged others to worship and obey the one God. As he gained converts in Mecca, he aroused suspicion and opposition among its leading families. In 622, thirteen years after the first *Call* (appearance of Gabriel), Muhammad and his followers moved to welcoming Yathrib, 218 miles (351 km) north of Mecca. This migration is known in Arabic as the *Hijra*. Yathrib later became known as Al-Madina (the City); we know it as Medina. Soon Muhammad became the ruler of Medina. He then conquered Mecca after an eight-year war, and established the Islamic faith in place of idol worship in western Arabia.

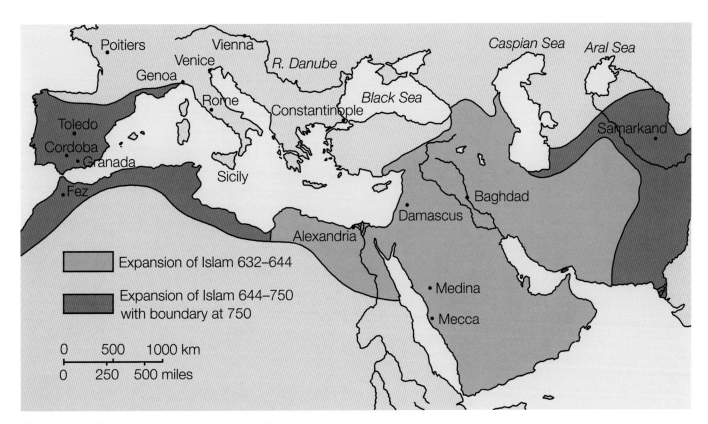

Figure 1.2 The spread of Islam into Europe.

The Muslims conquered North Africa between 670 and 708, Spain between 711 and 721, and Sicily during the 820s. The Christians recaptured Toledo in 1085, and much of southern Spain between 1212 and 1275. The Moors were not completely expelled from Granada until 1492. Sicily was captured by Normans between 1061 and 1091.

Based on the map in Bernard Lewis, *The Middle East* (London: Weidenfeld & Nicholson, 1995), pages 410–411.

Muhammad died in 632. He had not claimed to be other than mortal. He had restored the monotheism which had been taught by earlier prophets, abolished idolatry, and brought God's final revelation embodying the true faith and the Holy Law. He had barely started the task of taking Islam to the rest of the world. This role passed to his successors or khalifahs (caliphs). They continued Muhammad's forceful approach.

The Arab conquests began shortly after the Persian and Byzantine empires had just fought each other to exhaustion in a war lasting from 602 to 628. Both empires had greatly increased taxation to pay for the war. Their subjects did not strenuously oppose the opportunity to be ruled by lower-taxing Arabs.

In 636 or 637 the Sasanid army was first defeated by the Muslim caliph at the battle of Qadisiya. The whole of the Persian empire was conquered by 642. As a consequence the Arabs were exposed to chatrang, but called it *shatranj* because the Arabic alphabet does not have a *c* or a *g*. The Arabs called the chariot piece a rukh—the source of the modern term *rook*.

The earliest authenticated chessmen date from this period, but as they were excavated in Samarkand (earlier called Afrasiab), and are figurative carvings, not dissimilar to those in figure 1.8, they were unlikely to have been of Muslim manufacture.[2]

From Persia the Arabs continued to advance east into northwestern India, reaching the Indus river in 711. There Muslim troops encountered real war elephants for the first time.

The Arabs also drove west, taking shatranj with them. They finally captured Egypt from the Byzantines in 642. Arab armies then fought their way along the Barbary coast of North Africa against Byzantine armies and Berber tribes. The conquered Berbers converted to Islam, and together with Arabs continued the Islamic westward expansion. Lead by Tariq, who gave his name to Gibraltar (Jabal (Mount) Tariq), the Moors (the combination of Arabs with Berbers) crossed into Spain in 711. Toledo, the capital of the Christian Visigoth kingdom (*visi* means 'western') of the Franks, was captured in 712. Not until 732 was the Moors' northward advance halted at Poitiers by Charles Martel (his name lives on as a brand of cognac). As is described in the legends of figures 1.3 and 1.7, his grandson Charlemagne is associated, incorrectly, with chessmen.

ISLAM AND CHESS

Shatranj increased in popularity in Muslim countries during the ninth and tenth centuries despite opposition from those who saw it as timewasting and a distraction from religious observance. To counter this antipathy, adherents promoted the game as a serious pursuit and particularly a training for war, and wrote the first Arab books on shatranj.

The Arabs also developed non-figurative chessman designs in response to the Muslim stricture against figurative art. This stricture was so influential in the development of the design of chessmen that it will be explained in detail.

ISLAM AND ART

Islam demands that its practitioners submit themselves to the will of Allah (Arabic for God). A Muslim is one who has made that submission.[3] Muslims' action are thus governed by the Qur'an.

The Qur'an's text was insufficient to cover all possible situations, but because God had chosen Muhammad to deliver His message, Muslims came to believe that Muhammad's authentic words and actions were infallible. Although Muhammad did not claim infallibility outside the revelations in the Qur'an, his words and actions were remembered by those who had known him, and were handed down, at first orally. Known as *hadiths*, these remembrances were later collected, sorted into topics, and published for use.[4] Some of the earliest hadiths published were later believed to have been fabricated or exaggerated. The supposedly authentic hadiths were identified, and collections of them were published during the ninth century. The two most respected collections have an authority second only to the Qur'an; they also forbid figurative religious art

The Qur'an does not forbid figurative art, religious or secular. Its only relevant statement is: "O ye who believe, wine and games of chance and idols and divining arrows are an abomination of Satan's handiwork; so avoid it and prosper". This does not however forbid chess because chess is not a game of chance—it is a contest between two human intellects. Also, the idols referred to in the statement were pagan and included devices for the practice of sorcery—they did not include other figurative representations. Nevertheless, an antipathy to figurative imitation seems to have been latent in early Islamic religious thought, hardened during the century after Muhammad's death, and was incorporated into the collections of hadiths. This antipathy also evolved into the doctrine that because God was the great fashioner or shaper, those who shaped images in the form of living things were arrogating godlike powers to themselves.[5]

While the hadiths forbade figurative religious art, the involvement of religion in all Muslim life inevitably discouraged figurative secular art, although the imitation of non-figurative objects such as trees, other plants, and buildings was generally held to be permissible. Fortunately there were considerable regional and temporal variations in the antipathy to figurative secular art, and it is far from rare, in part because much of the art produced in Muslim regions was not produced by Muslims. The Muslim antipathy towards figurative art did however influence the design of chessmen. Therefore while figurative chessmen continued to be carved in Muslim-dominated regions (figure 1.3), the wish to avoid the figurative lead to the introduction of designs which were

1. Stylized imitations of figuratively carved chessmen (figure 1.4).
2. Abstract in form (see the pawn in figure 1.4, and all six pieces in figure 1.5). The designing of abstract chessmen probably developed later than and from the stylized imitations, perhaps starting with the pawns.

Determining when and where developments in the design of Arab and Muslim chessmen occurred and how the relative proportions of the three design types varied is impossible because so few chessmen earlier than A.D. 1000 have survived. Similarly the two following questions will probably remain unanswered

1. When were chessmen first made by turning? and how soon after before a significant proportion of chessmen were turned? Pawns were probably the first chessmen to be turned because they represented mere foot soldiers, and because there were sixteen pawns in a set. The lower cost of a turned chessman compared with carved thus resulted in a substantial cost saving on a set. This

Figure 1.3 An ivory king, eighth to tenth century, 6^1/$_8$ in. (156 mm) high. It was probably carved near Basra, Iraq.

This is one of the seventeen Charlemagne chessmen, so-called because they were long believed to have been a gift to Charlemagne (c. 742–814) by Harun al Raschid (765–809), Caliph of Baghdad. This chessman was made after Charlemagne's death, but earlier than the others, six of which are shown in figures 1.7 and 1.8.

Charlemagne was the grandson of Charles Martel, and the son of Pepin III, the Short. The soubriquet Charlemagne comes from Karolus called magnus (the elder), and was used to distinguish him from his own son, also named Charles.

Charlemagne was crowned Emperor of the Romans by Pope Leo III in St. Peter's, Rome, on Christmas Day 799. Charlemagne's continuing fame is largely due to the legends in the *Chansons de Geste*, a collection of about eighty medieval poems.

Bibliothèque nationale de France, Paris.

potential for cost saving was another factor which favored both the introduction and the growth in the popularity of stylized and abstract designs.

2. When was wood first used for chessmen? and how soon after before wood was used to make a significant proportion of chessmen? Although the earliest surviving chessmen are of rot-resistant ivory and bone, this does not extinguish the possibility that wooden chessmen might have been produced in significant numbers from early in the history of chess.

Turned wooden chess sets would have been much cheaper to produce than turned or carved sets in bone or ivory; and with cloth or leather boards would have been ideal for play during campaigning. Such combinations would have been the forerunners of the travelling sets with positively-locating men which were introduced in Europe in the second half of the eighteenth century.

Figure 1.4   Copies of stylized, Arab, bone chessmen from the eighth or ninth century in mulberry wood. The original king is 1⅝ in. (40 mm) tall. The original men are in the German National Museum, Nuremberg.

Notice the similarity of form of the king and queen to the king in the preceding figure. For both the mulberry king and queen: the projection on the top represents the mounted personage; the front part with the curved top represents an elephant's head; and the rest the elephant's body. The two projections on the bishop probably represent the tusks of the war elephant. The projection on the knight is far more likely to represent a horse's head than a shield. The rook's form may represent a horse-drawn chariot in profile.

The only source for the thick, dense bone used for these and other bone chessmen is the jaw bones of toothed whales. There are 70 species of toothed whale or *Odontocete*, which include the dolphins, porpoises, and the sperm whale which has a jaw bone up to 18 ft. (5.5 m) long. The 11 species of Baleen whale or *Mysticete* do not have jaw bones which are as dense.

The jaw bone is the only part of a toothed whale which offers dense bone through its whole thickness. Their other bones are cellular so that blood and marrow can circulate through them; they are therefore much like the enlarged ends of the limb bones of larger land mammals.

The bone chessmen which were commercially produced in large numbers in the nineteenth century would have been made from the jaw bones of sperm whales which were caught for their meat and the spermaceti oil and wax. The spermaceti organ in the huge head of a sperm whale enables the whale to dive to 6500 ft. (2000 m) at a rate of up to 500 ft. (150 m) per minute to catch squid.

Figure 1.5 Copies of abstract, Turkish, Muslim, eighteenth-century, colored-ivory pieces turned in Australian blackwood and Tasmanian oak. When such abstract designs were first produced for Muslim players is unknown. The originals are pictured in Alex Hammond, *The Book of Chessmen*, page 104.

1.4 MEDIEVAL EUROPE

The Arabs introduced chess into Byzantium, but the game did not spread westwards from there. There were three routes by which it may have been introduced into western Europe, although the first is likely to have been by far the most important:

1. Through Spain following the Muslim Moors' invasion of the Iberian Peninsular and the Narbonne area of France from Africa early in the eighth century (figure 1.2).
2. Into Italy, probably via the merchants of Venice and Genoa who traded with the Muslims of the Eastern Mediterranean.
3. Through Sicily. The Arabs progressively captured the island from the Byzantines during the 820s. Normans, descended from Vikings who had settled in northern France between 800 and 950, then took Sicily between 1061 and 1091, capturing Palermo in 1072, and thereby coming into contact with chess. These Normans may have taken chess back to northwest Europe only to find their relations already playing it.

By 1050 chess was played in all the European courts, displacing or coexisting with earlier board games. It was also increasingly played by the gentry and senior clergy. But the spread was not unopposed—its association with non-Christian Arabs partly explains the continued opposition from the Catholic church. Some of the Church hierarchy also regarded it as devilish because it was a game of the intellect. That it was typically played for a stake was also a negative. Not until about 1250 did Church opposition cease.

Written evidence for the presence of chess in Europe dates from the end of the eleventh century. Allegorical writings in which chess was used to illustrate themes of life were produced from the late Middle Ages (figure 1.6).

CHESSMEN

The Arab designs of chessmen taken into Western Europe would have been copied by the first European makers of chessmen. But European Catholics did not share the Islamic antipathy to figurative carving and decoration, and there was therefore a renaissance in the production of figuratively carved chessmen. During the Romanesque period as figures 1.7 and 1.8 show, figures and architectural ornament were increasingly carved into the basic Arab stylized forms similar to those in figure 1.4. The imitative carvers of chessmen broadened their subject matter during the Gothic period, and by 1300 chessmen were mimicking

**Figure 1.6   An illumination from the allegorical manuscript _Liber de moribus hominum et officiis
nobilium_** (Book of the Customs of Men and the Duties of Nobles) showing its author Jacobus de Cessolis
using chess to illustrate a sermon. Jacobo da Cessole (the vernacular version of his name) was a north-Italian
Dominican friar. He wrote the 20,000-word _Liber de moribus_ in Lombardy in about 1300 in Latin. It became
the most popular chess book of the Middle Ages. This is confirmed by the large number (about 200) of
manuscript copies which have survived, and by the printing between 1475 and 1505 of 20 editions in six
languages. William Caxton translated a French version into English and printed it (figure 1.15).

Cessolis did not explain how to play chess in _Liber de moribus_, but instead wrote an allegory in which he
used chess to symbolize aspects of contemporary medieval society, and thus advise and criticize without
being openly offensive. For example, he demonstrated that the rulers and the ruled were mutually dependent.
He equated roles in society to chess pieces so that laborers, smiths, masons, notaries, and others could be
likened to pawns: this was reflected in the practice of figuratively carving all the pawns in a set to imitate
different professionals and tradespeople.

La Trobe Collection, State Library of Victoria, Melbourne.

contemporary figures and objects rather than those associated with sixth-century Indian warfare. The carving was also an expressive outlet for designers and craftsmen, and a means of boasting and display by those who could afford these increasingly expensive sets.

While the application of carving grew, turning also became an increasingly important technique for making the chessmen for playing sets, which, as chess became more popular among the less wealthy, sold in increasing numbers.

The earliest extant European chessmen date from the eleventh and twelfth centuries (figures 1.7 to 1.12), the earliest extant turned set with examples of all six pieces is fourteenth century (figure 1.13).

Probably a vizier (there are also two kings each with a sceptre in the sixteen). Its back is semicircular in plan and architecturally carved. It is 4³/4 in. (122 mm) tall.

A queen piece carved to imitate a queen. The back of this chessman is also semicircular in plan and architecturally carved. It is 4³/4 in. (122 mm) tall.

Figure 1.7   Two of the sixteen Charlemagne chessmen carved from African ivory in the Amalfi region in southern Italy in the eleventh century; another four are shown in the next figure. The sixteen record the fighting between the Byzantine emperor Alexis Comnen I (1048–1118) and the Norman ruler Robert Quiscard (1014–1085). All are clothed in medieval robes and armor.

The king in figure 1.3 has been with the sixteen Amalfi-made men throughout their known history, but the carving on its base moldings is different to that on the other sixteen men, and it is much bigger; further evidence that it is from a different set.

Bibliothèque nationale de France, Paris.

A bishop carved to imitate a war elephant, 4$\frac{1}{4}$ in. (110 mm) tall..

A rook carved to imitate a chariot, 5 in. (126mm) tall.

A knight in medieval armor, 5 in. (127 mm) tall.

A pawn or footsoldier in medieval armor, 3 in. (76 mm) tall.

Figure 1.8 More of the sixteen Charlemagne Amalfi chessmen. The presence of an elephant and a chariot is remarkable. Alas, the origin of the chessmen which inspired the Amalfi carvers is unknown.

Figure 1.9   Resin replicas of a king, queen and knight of the Lewis chessmen. The seventy-eight chessmen are called the Lewis chessmen because they were unearthed on the Isle of Lewis in 1831.[6]

The original chessmen are late twelfth century, Viking in origin, between 2 and $4^1/2$ in. (50 and 115 mm) tall, and carved from walrus ivory either left natural or stained red.[7]

In this set the queen is definitely feminine, no longer the male vizier of shatranj. All the other Lewis pieces are similarly and instantly recognizable today, except for the rooks which are single foot soldiers with shields, much like the Charlemagne pawn in figure 1.8. There is no apparent connection between the Arab and Lewis rooks except that the sound of the Arabic *rukh* may have been confused with the Icelandic *hrokr* meaning 'brave soldier'. Some of the Lewis rook foot soldiers are shown biting their shields, a practice which the berserkers used to self-induce boldness and ferocity.[8] The berserkers were pre-medieval, Odin-worshipping shock troops. The term *Berserker* is Old Norse for 'bearskin'.

Photographed courtesy of Ken Raffe.

Figure 1.10   A Lewis bishop, height $3^5/8$ in. (93 mm). A medieval ecclesiastic has replaced the war elephant of shatranj. The points at the back and front of this Gothic miter have yet to climb to the extreme heights we associate with later Roman miters. The two streamers hanging from the back of the miter are lappets. Note the intricate carving to the back of the throne.

Reproduced from H. J. R. Murray, *A History of Chess*, Oxford University Press, p. 761.

Figure 1.11   Four Lewis pawns. Their forms imitate boundary stones, and their profiles resemble that of the Arab pawn in figure 1.4 .

Reproduced from H. J. R. Murray, *A History of Chess*, Oxford University Press, p. 763.

Figure 1.12   A late-twelfth-century, Nordic, bone bishop, knight, and rook copied in Australian rose mahogany. The originals are each about 1³/₈ in. (35 mm) tall, and are in the State Historical Museum, Stockholm,

Left. The power of medieval bishops was substantial enough for them to replace war elephants as supporters of the king in chess. Therefore war elephants could have been renamed bishops before the bishop's miter was adopted as the piece's symbol. Alternatively, the two horizontally projecting tusks of the war elephant of shatranj might have become upright because they were easier to turn and carve, were then seen to resemble a bishop's miter, and that lead to the renaming of the piece as a bishop and the adoption of the miter as its piece symbol.

Center. The knight remains similar to the Arab stylized version illustrated in figure 1.4.

Right. The upper part of the rook, while similar in elevation to the whole of an Arab rook, has ceased to imitate a chariot in elevation, and has become an ornamental plate of abstract design, perhaps because its origin as a chariot was unknown, and because the war chariot had not been used in Europe since the fourth century A.D. Whether the indented top later came to be thought to resemble battlements is unknown.

Figure 1.13 Copies of Scandinavian, fourteenth-century, bone chessmen turned in New Zealand beech. The original men are between 2 and 3 in. (50 and 76 mm) tall, and are in the Musée de Cluny, Paris.

The tops of the king, queen, and bishop may have been intended to resemble crowns and a miter respectively. The knight still resembles the Arab stylized form. The rook is probably too early to have been intended to resemble a castle tower. The pawn continues to retain an abstract form.

NAMING CHESSMEN

The Arab chess-piece names did not survive unchanged as Europeans adopted chess, and continued to change as the designs of European chessmen evolved. Not until the thirteenth century, however, did chess piece names enter the vocabularies of the European vernacular languages. Table 1.1 provides a guide to the European names for chess terms used through the centuries.

The conversion of the Arab vizier into a queen, rather than another notable, is of particular interest. In her book, *Birth of the Chess Queen*, Marilyn Yalom suggests that the presences of strong Medieval queens and consorts were influential.

CHESS BOARDS

Chess boards of one color have remained in use, particularly in Muslim countries, because they are not confusing to play on. European chess boards with bicolored squares were first recorded in 997 in the Einsiedeln Poem, written by a German-speaking monk, according to Marilyn Yalom (*Birth of the Chess Queen*, page 16). If these boards were introduced at that time, their bicoloring may have been copied from the checkered cloths used in rulers' financial departments or exchequers to display the movements of money. It is also, of course, possible that exchequer cloths derived their bicoloring from chess boards.[9]

NORTHEASTERN EUROPE AND RUSSIA

Chess spread into Byzantium during the ninth century, but was introduced into Russia from Persia and northern India, probably during the tenth century, by more-easterly land routes between the Black, Caspian, and Aral Seas. Figure 1.14 shows copies of medieval Russian chessmen.

| Table 1.1   A history of chess names. | | | | | | | |

Modern meaning	India 6th c.	Sasanid Persia	Early Islam	Europe pre-1200 Latin	Vernacular languages		
					English	French	German
Chess	Chaturanga	Chatrang	Shatranj	Esches (France) Scahzabel (Ger) Scachus or scaccus (Latin)	Chess	Échecs	Schach
King	Shah	Shah	Shah	Rex (king)	King	Roi	Konig
Queen	Wazir	Farzin	Firz, firzan (vizier)	Regina (queen) Femina (lady) Ferzia	Queen	Reine	Konigin
Bishop	Fil (elephant)	Pil	Fil alfil (elephant)	Comes (count) Senex, Calvus (Counsellor) Alphicus	Alfin Bishop	le dolphin (dauphin) le fou (fool or king's jester)	Laufer (runner)
Knight	Asp (cavalry)	Asp	Faras (horse)	Eques, caballarius, miles (all mean knight).	Knight	Cavalier	Springer
Rook	Rukh (chariot)	Rukh (chariot)	Rukh, rukhkh, rokh (chariot)	Rochus Marchio (marquess)	Rook	Tour	Turm
Pawn	Piyada (foot soldier)	Pujada	Baidaq	Pedes	Pawn	Pion	Bauer

Table 1.1   A history of chess names. This table is largely based on tables 1 and 2 in Richard Eales, *Chess: the History of a Game*. It shows that today's European terms for *chess* are derived from *shah*, not from *shatranj*.

The piece names first used by Europeans had three sources:

1. When the meaning of the Arab piece name was understood and had a European equivalent, the European equivalent term was likely to be adopted.

2. When the Arab term was not understood, its sound was sometimes adopted, although meaningless, because chess-piece names do not have to have any association with real persons or objects. For example, in England a bishop was called an *alfin* although elephants had not been seen in Europe since Hannibal's invasion of 218 B.C.[10] Subsequently, because the alfins were positioned close to the king, they came to be regarded as the king's counsellors who were usually bishops in medieval times.

3. When the Arab term was phonetically similar to an existing European vernacular name, the latter often displaced the former. Thus the Arabic *alfil* was replaced by *le fol* (fool) or initially le *dolphin* (dauphin) in France, *alfiere* (standard bearer) in Italian; and *laufer* (runner) in German.

Figure 1.14 Copies of Russian bone chessmen from the thirteenth to fifteenth centuries, turned in jarrah and camphor laurel. The men are from different sets, and the originals are pictured in I. M. Linder, *The Art of Chess Pieces*, pages 234, 238, 230, 178, 226, and 237 respectively.

The original men might have been carved from the jawbones of beluga whales which live in the Caspian and Black seas.

1.5 RENAISSANCE EUROPE

The second book William Caxton printed was *The Game and Playe of the Chesse Moralised.*[11] When he printed it again five years later in 1480 after transferring from Bruges to London, it was only the second book printed in England with moveable type (figures 1.15 and 1.16). The earliness of these printings is but one demonstration that chess was widely played by Europe's educated during the Renaissance.

The chess played in Europe during the early Renaissance period was essentially still the shatranj form imported by the Arabs, but between 1470 and 1490 the more aggressive game we play today was developed, probably in Spain and/or Portugal. Pawns could henceforth advance two squares on their first move, not one; and the bishop and queen were given their greater, present powers of movement. The new chess spread rapidly, and had almost totally displaced the shatranj form in Europe by the middle of the sixteenth century. One of the earliest descriptions of the new chess was given in a book by Luis de Lucena, printed in 1496 or 1497 in Salamanca, Spain (figure 1.18). *Liber de moribus* was also among the earliest European books which described how to play chess.

CHESSMEN

The designs of chessmen developed and multiplied greatly through the Renaissance period. These changes were not orderly, in part because most of those who made chessmen did not play chess or understand the symbolism of chess-piece designs. The introduction (or possibly reintroduction, as it may have been in use in Roman times) of the two-bearing lathe headstock at around the end of the fifteenth century catalyzed the introduction of more-elaborately turned men. While carved sets continued to be made, turned playing sets with little carving were made in increasing numbers.

The number of extant men, especially from early in this period is small (figure 1.17). We are fortunate, however, that H. J. R. Murray searched contemporary manuscripts and printed books, and reproduced the illustrations he found on pages 769 to 774 of A *History of Chess*. Most of the original illustrations are crude, and therefore show playing-pieces which are sometimes of unlikely form. The relative sizes of some of the pieces are also unlikely. Figures 1.18 to 1.23 show some of Murray's illustrations or my interpretations of them.

Figure 1.15   A plate from *The Game and Playe of the Chesse* showing the philosopher Xerxes teaching a king to play chess. The book is William Caxton's translation and printing of Cessolis's moralizing manuscript *Liber de moribus hominum et officiis nobilium* (figure 1.6). In it Cessolis asserted that chess had been invented by a philosopher named Xerxes who Cessolis confused with the Persian emperor of the same name who had lived between 519 and 465 B.C.

Caxton (c. 1422–1491) learned printing in Cologne between 1470 and 1472. He set up a press in Bruges in 1474, and in that year printed the first book in English, *The Recuyell* (Recall) *of the Historyes of Troye,* which he had translated from the French. Caxton next printed, probably in 1475 and without woodcuts, *The Game and Playe of the Chesse Moralised*. Late in 1476 Caxton returned to England, and established England's first press at Westminster. The first book he printed there was *Dictes and sayenges of the Phylosophers*, published on November 18, 1477. In 1480 he printed a second book, a second edition of *The Game and Playe of the Chesse* which this time was illustrated with woodcuts.

La Trobe Collection, State Library of Victoria, Melbourne.

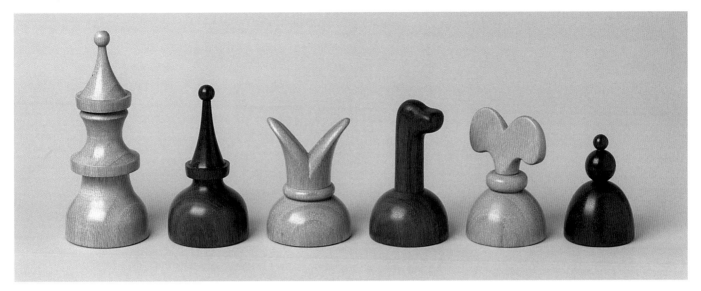

Figure 1.16   Chess pieces based on woodcuts in Caxton's *The Game and Playe of the Chesse*, in paperbark and Queensland walnut; they are copied from the illustration on page 770 of H. J. R. Murray, *A History of Chess*. These pieces show graduation in height, approximately from king down to pawn; a bishop with a divided top resembling a miter; a knight with probably a stylized horse's head; a two-lobed rook; and a simple pawn with a top incorporating two spheres.

While book illustrations from the sixteenth century are usually crude, the seventeenth-century books by the Duke of Brunswick-Lüneburg and Thomas Hyde have excellent illustrations of German, Indian, and Turkish chessmen (figures 1.23 to 1.28). Another source for illustrations of contemporary chess equipment are the paintings and drawings which show chess being played.

The development of European names and symbols for chess pieces has been introduced. How the castle tower became the symbol for the rook is the least certain. An instruction for fashioning pieces in the largely Muslim Spanish Alfonso MS of 1283 confirms the bishop as an elephant with a howdah.[12] Perhaps the desire to develop a less labor-intensive symbol for the rook lead to the dismissal of the elephant and the conversion of its howdah into a castle tower. Another possibility is that the rook became a castle tower because rukh sounded similar to rocco, Italian for tower.

The Latin poem *De Ludo scaccorum* (The Game of Chess) by Marcus Hieronymous Vida of Cremona, Bishop of Alba, is sometimes cited as being influential in the adoption of the castle tower. Vida's poem describes a chess contest between Apollo and Mercury using invented "classical" names for the pieces. Vida's word for rook was Elephas, after Livy who refers in his *History of Rome* to elephants bearing towers. This perhaps lead to the practice of carving rooks in the form of a square tower on an elephant (figure 1.25). It was then only a short step to dismiss the elephant and round the tower's corners off in the lathe. However, although Vida's poem was first drafted in 1510, it was not published until about 1525 (in Lyons), just after the publication of the first printed image of a castle-tower rook in Damiano's 1524 book (figure 1.21). While this suggests that the tower form was not derived from Vida's 658-line poem, the poem became hugely popular (by 1616 forty printed editions in Latin and other languages had been published), and may have helped to popularize the adoption of the castle tower.

Another possibility is that the castle tower was adopted because some medieval battlement merlons resemble the Arab stylized rook (compare figures 1.4 and 3.33). While this possibility is remote, by the middle of the seventeenth century the symbols we use today to denote the six chess pieces were already in use, and conditions were ripe for chess to grow rapidly.

Figure 1.17 Copies of chess pieces (K, Q, N, R, P) made by Baldassarre Embriachi in Florence in about 1450. The wood is Honduras mahogany.

The white men of the original set (which is incomplete) are bone, the black men are horn. They and the magnificent accompanying board are in the Ashmolean Museum, Oxford, and are pictured in color in Colleen Schaffroth, *The Art of Chess*, pages 88 to 89, and Gareth Willams, *Master Pieces*, pages 27 and 30. The Embriachi family of carvers are discussed in Novello Williams, "A Prince of Carvers, A Carver to Princes", *The Chess Collector*, Autumn 2000, pages 10 to 12.

Figure 1.18 Copies of chess pieces pictured in 1497 in Luis de Lucena's *Repetición de amores e arte de axedrez con cl iuegos de partido* (A Discourse on Love and Chess).

The king and queen have different crowns. The top of the bishop may imitate a bishop's cap. The knight is represented by a horse's head.

These copies in Burdekin plum and rock maple are based on the illustration in H. J. R. Murray, *A History of Chess*, page 770.

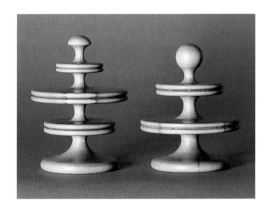

Figure 1.19 Copies of a king and queen pictured in 1512 in *Questo libro e da imparare giocare a scachi et de le partite* by Portuguese apothecary Damiano. After the first printing in Rome, another six editions were published there in the next 50 years. French, English, and German translations were also published.

This king and queen are the earliest pieces pictured with forms consisting of disks spaced on a thin stem, with the number of disks being used to distinguish the type of piece.

These sassafras copies are based on the illustration in H. J. R. Murray, *A History of Chess*, page 770.

Figure 1.20 Pieces pictured in 1520 in Kobel's German, Oppenheim, edition of Jacob Mennel's *Schachzabel*, an abbreviated version of 586 lines of Kunrat von Ammenhausen's version of Cessolis' *Liber de moribus* (figure 1.6). Similar piece forms are repeated in woodcuts in a book published in 1520 by Dr. V. Mennol (almost certainly the same person as Mennel) shown in Gareth Williams, *Master Pieces*, page 31.

The king and queen feature battlements instead of crowns with points. Could the head of the bishop imitate the top of a thumb stick if this feature were used for bishops crosiers? (Crosiers are first mentioned as a sign of a bishop's ruling power in 633, and were gradually adopted throughout Christendom). Another possibility is that the bishop's head imitates two serpents facing each other, a feature sometimes found on the tops of crosiers of bishops of the Eastern churches. Finally, could the head of the knight be an imitation of a knight's saddle or stirrup?

Reproduced from H. J. R. Murray, *A History of Chess*, page 771.

 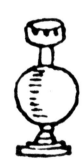    

Figure 1.21 Pieces pictured in 1524 in the fifth Rome edition of Damiano's book *Questo libro* (pieces from the first edition are shown in figure 1.19). The rook is the first-known imitation of a castle tower. The spherical parts of the king, queen, and bishop perhaps presage the use of spheres in the later basic French design of the eighteenth and nineteenth centuries (figures 1.31 and 1.32).

Reproduced from H. J. R. Murray, *A History of Chess*, page 771.

Figure 1.22 Copies of chess pieces pictured in 1536 in Egenolff's Frankfurt edition of *Schachzabel*, itself a version of Cessolis' *Liber de moribus*. These Honduras mahogany copies are based on the illustration in H. J. R. Murray, *A History of Chess*, page 770.

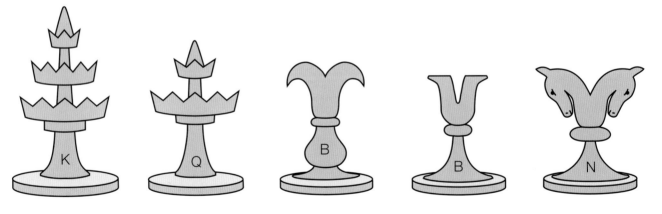

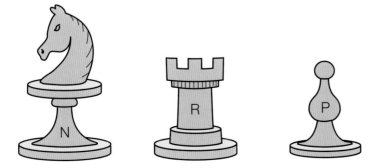

Figure 1.23 Playing chessmen pictured in 1616 in Germany. The stacked crowns of the kings and queens, the castle-tower rooks, and the horse-head knights, both single and double, are by now well established.

Chessmen with stacked crowns or similar are now called *Selenus* after the author of the book detailed in the legend of the next figure.

Based on drawings in H. J. R. Murray, *A History of Chess*, page 771.

Figure 1.24 An engraving from the book commonly known as *Selenus* showing its author, Augustus, Duke of Brunswick-Lüneburg (1579–1666), playing chess. The Duke is seated on the right. This illustration is taken from pages 216 and 217 of *Schach-oder Königspiel* (Chess or the King Game) published in Leipzig in 1616. The Duke's use of the nom de plume Gustavus Selenus suggests that he was not trying too hard to hide his authorship because Gustavus is an anagram of Avgustus, Selenus was the Greek goddess of the moon, and luna is Latin for moon, which ties back to Lüneburg.

The book was the first instructional chess book in German. Its text partly follows that of *Libro de la invención liberal y arte del juego del Axedrez* published in 1561 in Alcalá, Spain, by Spanish priest Ruy López de Segura. *Selenus* is also exceptional for its illustrations of contemporary central-European chessmen (figures 1.23 and 1.25).

La Trobe Collection, State Library of Victoria, Melbourne.

The king.

The queen.

The man (bishop).

The intriguer (jester, bishop).

A messenger (knight).

A marksman (knight).

A rook.

A rider (a rook not a knight).

A soldier (pawn).

Figure 1.25   Nine figurative chess pieces pictured in *Selenus* on one double page. Each carving is supported on one of five designs of turned baluster pedestal. Note particularly the rook in the form of an elephant carrying a tower.

La Trobe Collection, State Library of Victoria, Melbourne.

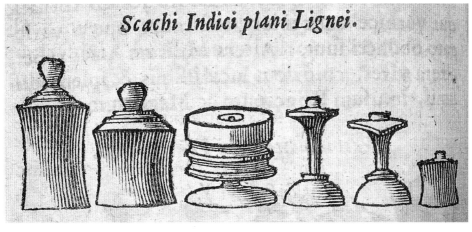

Scachi Indici plani Lignei.

Scachi Indici plani Eburnei solidi.

Scachi Indici plani Eburnei cavi.

Figure 1.26   Turned, Indian Muslim chessmen pictured in 1694 in part 2 of Thomas Hyde's *De Ludis Orientalibus* (an earlier part was published in 1689). Written in Latin, the book was a history of oriental games.

These sets had been bought in Surat or Bombay by a Sir D. Sheldon and given to Hyde. Their turned designs have continued in production with little variation to the present. The facetting used on the pieces second from the right in the top two sets was used on some eighteenth and nineteenth-century French bishops (figures 1.31). The bottom "cavi" pieces are excavated or hollowed, and each contained a bell, perhaps to enable musical chess or prevent surreptitious moves.

Hyde (1636-1702) was from 1665 until his death chief librarian at the Bodleian Library. He was appointed a professor of Arabic at Queen's College, Oxford, in 1691, and of Hebrew in 1697. Hyde was the first to promote the idea that chess had been invented in India. He also explained the origin of *check mate*: *check* was from *shah*, *mate* was from the Persian word *mat* meaning 'to remain', i.e. exhausted or conquered and unable to move.[13]

La Trobe Collection, State Library of Victoria, Melbourne.

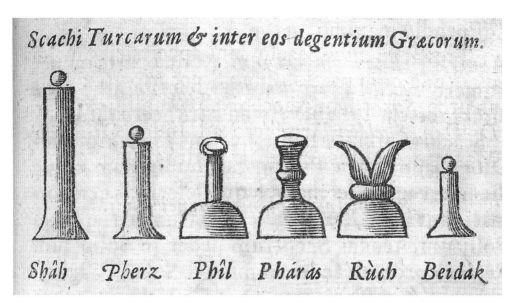

Figure 1.27   Turned Turkish pieces pictured in Thomas Hyde's book. The rook resembles the European bishops pictured by Caxton (figure 1.16) and Selenus (figure 1.23).
        La Trobe Collection, State Library of Victoria, Melbourne.

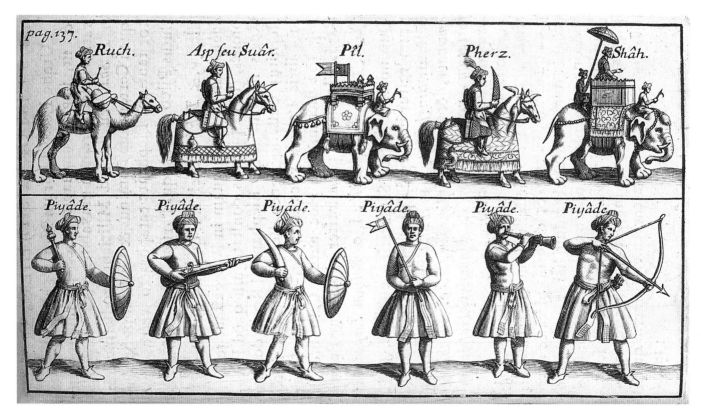

Figure 1.28   Indian, Hindu, figurative chessmen pictured in Thomas Hyde's book. The pieces of the top row are, *left to right*, rook, knight, bishop, queen, and king. The rukh is a cavalryman mounted on a camel. Along the bottom row, each of the pawns is differently armed. The practice in carved sets of having each pawn a different variation on the theme was also used in Europe.
        La Trobe Collection, State Library of Victoria, Melbourne.

1.6 EUROPE, 1650–1800

Between 1650 and 1800 chess ceased to be a casual game for aristocratic amateurs, and developed into a serious intellectual pursuit with a growing technical literature and rising standards of play. The number of chess players grew strongly, and many chess sets have survived, particularly from later in the period. In 1650 Spain and Italy were the leading chess nations. By 1800 France dominated and England had progressed to second.

As the social appeal of chess waned in the great households early in the eighteenth century, chess players began to meet and play regularly in the clubs, cafés, and coffee houses which were springing up. Cafés served food and drink to short-staying clients; coffee houses (which served food and other beverages in addition to coffee) encouraged their patrons to dally, and thus became centers for business, bandinage, and chess. London's first coffee house opened in 1652.[14] In Paris, the Café de la Régence had by 1750 become a Mecca for chess players.[15] Among its later frequenters was Robespierre[16]— perhaps he was unaware that the Café was named after Philippe II, duc d'Orléans who had owned the site of the Café and been regent of France for the young Louis XV between 1715 and 1723.

The clubs and coffee houses were also where the few chess professionals plied their trade. The most important of these during the second quarter of the eighteenth century was Philip Stamma. Born in Syria, he arrived in Paris in the 1730s. In 1737 he published his *Essai sur le Jeu des Échecs*. Shortly after he acquired a patron, Lord Harrington, and moved to England. There he was later to play Francois André Danican Philidor (1726–1795), pictured in figure 1.29.

PHILIDOR

In 1745 Philidor, then nineteen, went to Holland on a musical appointment. It fell through. The stranded Philidor resorted to playing checkers (draughts) and chess with English officers there for the War of the Austrian Succession. Because of his great prowess, they encouraged him to go to England, which he did in 1747. Slaughter's Coffee House in St Martin's Lane, London, established in 1692, was a major chess venue.[17] At Slaughter's stakes were raised for him to play Stamma. Philidor won convincingly, and was

Figure 1.29   Philidor pictured in the engraved frontispiece of his book *L'Analyze des Echecs*.

Philidor was born near Paris into a family of court musicians. He followed his family's musical calling with some success, but derived much of his income from chess which he had learnt when a child.

Philidor was a major force in increasing chess's popularity through his chess writings, and through public play and exhibitions in France, Germany, and England.

La Trobe Collection, State Library of Victoria.

thenceforth regarded as the best player of the time.

In 1748 Philidor returned to Holland and there wrote L'*Analyze des Echecs*, first published in London in 1749. Editions in English and German soon followed. Philidor's book was successful because it gave more thorough and complete advice to players in a brief and lucid way. In 1751 Philidor went to Germany and played before Frederick the Great.

Philidor then resumed his musical career, but in 1771 returned to London to publish revised and expanded editions of L'*Analyze des Echecs* with Charles Burney providing the translation for the English edition. The 280 subscribers from both Britain and France included thirteen dukes, and notable intellectuals such as Voltaire, Gibbon, and Diderot.

At this time chess was at it's most fashionable, and nowhere more so than at Parsloe's Subscription Room in St James's Street, London (figure 1.30). Its membership was limited to one hundred, and the annual subscription was three guineas. Probably in 1774 "several zealous Members made a subscription among themselves, in order to defray Mr Philidor's expenses, and enable him to attend them during the winter" which he did from February to May each year.[18]

The French revolution started in 1789. A war between Britain and France followed. Philidor was unable to return to Paris in 1793, was forced to remain in London, and died there in August 1795.

Figure 1.30   Philidor playing blindfold before the Turkish ambassador at Parsloe's Subscription Room, an engraving from the *Sporting Magazine* of 1793 or 1794. In such exhibitions two or three opponents were played simultaneously. The first recorded blindfolded player was a negro, Sa'id Bin Jubair who died in 714.[19] Chess playing declined at Parsloe's after Philidor's death in 1795. The club closed in 1825.

Reproduced from Fred Wilson, *A Picture History of Chess*, page 17.

1.61 CHESSMEN

The size and number of workshops which specialized in making chess sets grew through the period. There was no standardization of chess set designs, although particular designs predominated in different regions.

Chessmen varied greatly in elaboration and cost, with the cheapest sets being turned in wood. In the clubs and coffee houses where chessmen were liable to receive rougher usage than in homes, wooden playing sets were the norm. Playing sets with larger-than-usual men were ordered by clubs for exhibition matches.

Elaborately carved displaying sets were made in Europe, and were increasingly imported from China and the Indian subcontinent by Western trading companies, especially the English East India Company. This company, formed in 1600 as The Company of Merchants of London Trading into the East Indies, established factories in India at Vizagapatam at the end of the seventeenth century. Chess sets for the European market were made there, some based on English designs. As the English East India Company was familiarily called the John Company, sets exported by it from Asia are called John sets.

CHESSMEN IN FRANCE

To cater for the increasing demand from the French and other national markets, the first craft workshops to produce chess sets in large numbers were started in France, notably in Paris, Lyons, and Dieppe.

The basic eighteenth- and nineteenth-century French turned playing set was made in many variations (figures 1.31 and 1.32); and mainly in wood, in bone, and in wood with bone ornamentation. Three names are given to this family of turned playing sets:

1. *Directoire*—the twentieth-century American appellation. The name is usually applied to the simpler decorative arts style, partly influenced by the discoveries at Pompeii, fashionable in France between the 1789 Revolution and the end of the eighteenth century.
2. *Régence* (often Anglicized to *Regency*)—for chess sets based on the name of the Café de la Régence, but more commonly applied to the decorative arts style fashionable between 1800 and 1830, before and during the regency of Philip, duc d'Orleans. It was transitional between the massive rectilinear style of Louis XIV and the Rococo style of Louis XV.
3. *Lyons*—another twentieth-century appellation, recalling the French city, and reserved for sets where the wooden men have bone ornamentation.

CHESSMEN IN BRITAIN

Late in the eighteenth century, companies specializing in the manufacture of chess sets were started in England, notably in London. The best-known include Calvert (c. 1790–c. 1840), Hastilow, Jaques (1795–), and Lund. Also late in the eighteenth century, makers started to label their chess products, a practice for which today's collectors are grateful.

Although self-employed craftsmen continued to make sets which did not conform to a defined style (figure 1.33 and 1.34), during the second half of the eighteenth century, three patterns became established in Britain, and continued to be manufactured into the twentieth century:

1. The *basic French* style was imported from France, but it was also made in Britain and in other Western-European countries.
2. The *old-English* or *English pattern* has kings and queens with the overall form of an upwardly tapering tower consisting of convex and concave parts (figure 1.35). The men were usually turned in one piece in wood or bone. The *St. George* pattern was a version of the old-English which developed in the nineteenth century, characterized by a king with an overly-large crown surmounted by a squashed orb and a cross patée (figure 1.48).
3. The *barleycorn* pattern has a king and queen of approximately old-English form each supported on a relatively slim baluster on a disk-like base (figures 1.36 and 1.43). The men were usually bone, and were assembled from component parts which screwed together.

CHESSMEN IN EUROPE

The Selenus-style stacks of crowns continued to feature in many of the more ornately turned sets made in Germany, Austria, and Italy (figure 1.37).

Figure 1.31   French, eighteenth-century, turned pieces in boxwood and walnut. King 3³⁄₈ in. (86 mm) tall.

The French called their bishop a *fou* meaning 'court jester'. The easily turned and carved bishop's miter was not therefore employed. To give greater differentiation the top of the fou was often facetted. The forms of the bishop and knight are sometimes confused because the bishop is the shorter. Whether the large, low bulbs of the six pieces vary in form only to aid differentiation, I don't know.

The design was widely promoted to turners, For example, drawings of almost identical pieces are shown in figures 39 to 44, plate XXV, Volume 1 of Louis-Eloy Bergeron, *Manuel du Tourneur*, published 1792, second edition 1816.

Polumbaum Collection. Photograph Risa Korris.

Figure 1.32   Men of the French basic design similar to that in the preceding figure, but with horse-head knights. This set was made much later than that in the preceding figure.

Figure 1.33   English chessmen and their chess table, early seventeenth-century. Turned in beech and ash, the black side was stained. The men are unusually tall with the king being 12 in. (305 mm) high. The table-top board is pine, 3ft. 5in. (1040 mm) square, and the squares are 4¹/₂ in. (114 mm) across. The table underframing may have been fixed to the board later.

   The men and table are described in Edward H. Pinto, *Treen and Other Wooden Bygones* (London: G. Bell & Sons, 1969), pages 217 to 218, and plate 235.

   Pinto collection, Birmingham Museum & Art Galleries.

Figure 1.34 A set made in Ireland in the late eighteenth century in stained and unstained arbutus wood. A vaguely similar set is pictured in Gareth Williams, *Master Pieces*, pages 54 and 55. The ribbon signifies that the piece is a bishop. The set was probably made as a souvenir.

There are twenty species in the *Arbutus* genus. *Arbutus unedo* is native to Ireland, and is commonly called the strawberry tree because its fruits resemble small strawberries.

Polumbaum Collection. Photograph Risa Korris.

Figure 1.35 Copies of eighteenth-century English pieces. The originals are pictured in Michael Mark, *British Chess Sets*, 2nd Edition, exhibit 1. The king and queen are primitive precursors of the barleycorn pattern; the other pieces of a style later called English pattern. The knight is "cut aslant". The wood is river oak, *Casuarina cunninghamiana*. Three pieces are stained black.

Figure 1.36 Copies in New Zealand beech of pieces from an English, *circa* **1770, ivory, barleycorn set** pictured in Gareth Williams, *Master Pieces*, pages 40 and 41. An identical set was owned by President George Washington (1732–1799), and is displayed in the United States National Museum, Washington. The bases in these copies have been thickened by the addition of a bead and fillet. The black side of the original set was stained red, the white side was unstained. A nineteenth-century barleycorn set is shown later in figure 1.43.

Figure 1.37 An Italian, bone set with stacked crowns and helmeted bishops, late eighteenth or early nineteenth century. The king is 3¹/₈ in. (79 mm) tall.
Polumbaum Collection. Photograph Risa Korris.

1.7 THE NINETEENTH CENTURY

During the early part of the nineteenth century, Paris and London shared the chess limelight, but it shifted to London after Howard Staunton became the first "world champion" in 1843 (his contributions to British chess are discussed in the legend to figure 1.45). Staunton conceived and organized the first International Chess Tournament with prizemoney of £500 to coincide with London's 1851 Great Exhibition at the Crystal Palace. Thereafter master players from different countries played one another increasingly often; they were also more likely to become full-time professionals and media personalities.

By the end of the nineteenth century chess was played not just in Europe, but throughout the world, even if in many regions only among the wealthy and the ruling classes. Islamic invaders and traders had taken chess into Southeast Asia, the East Indies, and Africa (figure 1.38). Europeans had taken chess to the Americas, and Australasia.

The manufacture of Western-style chessmen also spread, notably to North America, India, and China, but remained concentrated in Europe.

EUROPEAN CHESSMEN

The making of chessmen by self-employed craftsmen and by specialist companies flourished throughout Europe in the nineteenth century. Designs from previous centuries were modified to accord with the fashion changes in the decorative arts, and the plainer designs popular at the start of the century (figure 1.39) were displaced by fussier ones (figures 1.40 and 1.41).

Although materials which can be molded to shape are better for mass manufacture, ceramic chessmen were too fragile for playing sets; and although metal chessmen could be both durable and cheap, they were not significantly cheaper then than chessmen turned and carved from the still-plentiful ebony, box, other preferred woods, whale jawbone, and African ivory. Perhaps players also preferred the tactile properties of materials which grew, and appreciated the presence of hand workmanship.

The nineteenth century is properly associated with the railways, the building of which started to boom in the 1840s in Europe.[20] People travelled more often and more smoothly than they had in horse-drawn coaches. Travelling chess sets therefore became popular (figure 1.42).

Figure 1.38 Copies of the ivory chess pieces given by Welled Selasse, the Ras of Tigre, to Henry Salt (1780–1827) in 1805 when Salt visited Abyssinia (now Ethiopia). One side was originally stained red, the other side was unstained. The original men are now in the British Museum, London.

The turnings are copied from the drawing in H. J. R. Murray, *A History of Chess*, page 363. The black pieces are in Queensland Walnut, the white in bluestained Moreton Bay fig.

Figure 1.39 Plainer-style, Austrian, early-nineteenth-century, Biedermeier pieces in boxwood and an unknown darker wood. The king is 3 in. (76 mm) high.

The Biedermeier style was a more comfortable version of the French Empire style of decorative arts, and was popular among the bourgeoisie of Germany and Austria during the first half of the nineteenth century. The appellation is derived from Biedermann and Bummelmeier, two characters in a Berlin journal which satirized bourgeois philosophy.

Polumbaum Collection. Photograph Risa Korris.

Figure 1.40 An ornate, 1889 chess-set design for German woodturners reproduced from the pattern book *Musterblätter moderner Drechslerarbeiten* by A. Graef and M. Graef, reprinted Hannover: Verlag Th. Schafer, 1982.

Figure 1.41   An intricate,1895, chess-set design for German woodturners reproduced from the 1895 *Musterblätter moderner Drechslerarbeiten*, by A. Graef and M. Graef, reprinted Hannover: Verlag Th. Schafer, 1982.

Figure 1.42   A travelling chess set, the Whittington. It was made by the London company John Jaques between about 1890 and 1930 from bone and wood.

Maryhill Museum of Art, Goldendale, Washington, USA. The Museum has an extensive collection of chess sets.

CHESSMEN IN BRITAIN

The Industrial Revolution started in Britain in about 1770. It, together with associated developments in health and agriculture, lead to rapid increases in population and urbanization. The middle classes who had wealth, education, and leisure time also grew strongly in numbers, so therefore did the number of chess players.

The basic British chess set designs of the eighteenth century continued to be made during the nineteenth, often with increased ornateness (figure 1.43). Some designs lacked stability, and the pieces of some were difficult to differentiate under the poor artificial lighting of the time, especially after an imbibition of claret and port. Chess set manufacturers therefore sought to develop more-functional designs even before the post-1851-Great-Exhibition revolt against excessive ornament. These improved designs were also more durable, cheaper to make, and were intended to be distinguishable from the designs of competitors. A spur was the introduction in 1842 of design registration which allowed designs to become intellectual property. This in turn encouraged pictorial advertizing and catalogues because the sets illustrated could no longer be copied without the risk of court action.

Although chessmen were still carved and turned by hand, the manufacturers strove to achieve accurate conformance to their standard designs. Workmanship was still relatively cheap, but the number of skilled, innately-artistic carvers was inevitably small. With training, the ability to replicate designs on a lathe can be gained by a much higher percentage of workers, hence the manufacturers' focus on turned designs with restricted carving (figure 1.44). Highly carved sets were still made in Britain, but an increasing proportion were imported from India and China.

Figure 1.43   Men from a nineteenth-century, English, barleycorn, bone set. A carved flag originally projected from the top of the rook. This design is called barleycorn because on some sets with forms similar to this, two bands of short helical grooves were carved around the center of the drums of the king and queen. The slope of one band of grooves was opposed to the slope of the other, and the resulting ornament resembles the grain-bearing top (ear or corn) of barley.

Figure 1.44   An old-English playing set and box made by J. Calvert of 189 Fleet Street, London, about 1830. The woods used for the men are a rosewood (*Dalbergia* species) and boxwood. The king is 4³/₄ in. high, the box is 11 in. (280 mm) long x 7 ¹/₂ in. (190 mm) wide x 5 ¹/₈ in. (130 mm) high.
   Courtesy of Garrick Coleman, London.

THE STAUNTON DESIGN

Howard Staunton, England's first world chess champion (figure 1.45), allowed his name to be appended to the most successful new chess set design of the nineteenth century (figure 1.46). Although not revolutionary in its design, its sales soon exceeded those of competing designs (figure 1.47), and it remains dominant even today.

The design was registered on 1st March 1849 under the Ornamental Designs Act 1842 as an "Ornamental Design for a Set of Chess-Men" by one Nathaniel Cook of 198, Strand. The firm of John Jaques first advertised the set for sale on 29th September 1849. The exact natures and timings of the involvements of Cook, Jaques, and Staunton in the set's genesis is unknown.[21]

The Staunton pattern has simplicity, and clarity—the king is represented by an arched crown, the queen by a pointed crown without arches or pearls (see page 73). The men are also unusually stable because their bottoms are relatively wide, and because their bases are *leaded* (bored, and filled with lead metal).

DESIGNS FOR SMALLER MARKETS

Before the late eighteenth century, most chess set designs had been restricted to particular regions because of isolation and the absence of manufacturers and retailers with an international focus. In the nineteenth century the new, larger companies sought extra turnover and profit by targetting international and national markets (figure 1.48), and smaller markets such as particular regions and even individual chess venues and clubs (figures 1.49 and 1.50). Thus, for example, the firm of Jaques, among the largest English manufacturers of quality chess sets, produced a considerable number of different designs (figures 1.50 to 1.55).

Figure 1.45 Howard Staunton (1810–1874). He beat the world's leading player, Frenchman Pierre de St. Amant, at the Café de la Régence in Paris in 1843, and became acknowledged as the first world champion.

Staunton did much to popularize chess in Britain. He founded the first chess magazine in English in 1841. He wrote the hugely successful *The Chess Player's Handbook*, first published in 1847, which ran to 21 editions, the last published in 1939. His later books were *Chess Player's Companion*, first published in 1849; *The Chess Tournament* in 1852; and *Chess Praxis* in 1860. He wrote a chess column in the *Illustrated London News* from 1845 until his death. But Staunton's name is immortalized not for these accomplishments, or for his Shakespearian scholarship, but through the Staunton chessmen which are named after him. Staunton actively promoted the design, his signature was on the label on the molded box of Gothic design (designed by Joseph L. Williams and manufactured in carton pierre), and he received a royalty on sales.

Figure 1.46   Men of a Staunton club set made in ivory by Jaques *circa* 1865. The king is 5¹/₂ in. (140 mm) tall. The design of these knights is more vigorous than those of later versions (figure 1.59). The American company The House of Staunton is currently reproducing this early design.
    Courtesy of Garrick Coleman, London.

Figure 1.47   Copies of Philidor pieces. Named after the eighteenth century's leading player, and manufactured by G. Merrifield of Lincoln's Inn-fields, London, these men were designed for durability (page 93).
    Staunton, whose royalties would have been adversely affected by any sales which the Philidor took from the Staunton design, wrote in 1851 in response to a letter, "We quite agree with you that of the new designs for chess pieces which the success of the "Staunton men" has brought to light, those called the "Philidor Chessmen" are the least to be commended. Instead of being an improvement on the old pieces, they are still more outré [passing the bounds of what is usual and considered proper] in shape, and with no one quality of usefulness to redeem their want of beauty".

Figure 1.48 Pieces of a St. George set in box and ebony, leaded and of unusually large size (the king 5$^{1}/4$ in. (133 mm) high). This large-crowned variant of the English-pattern was popular in England during the first half of the nineteenth century, and was named after England's patron saint—there wasn't any association with the St George's chess club in Hanover Square, London, which was founded in 1843.[22]

Polumbaum Collection. Photograph by Risa Korris.

Figure 1.49 The Northern Upright or Edinburgh pattern, designed by Lord John Hay, probably in the early 1840s. It was popular in Scotland, and manufactured by Jaques until early in the twentieth century. Another variant has upward-tapering column shafts (figure 1.52).[23]

Polumbaum Collection. Photograph by Risa Korris.

Figure 1.50   Copies of the chess pieces designed in 1828 by Jaques for the Grand Cigar Divan, the most important chess venue in London in the second quarter of the nineteenth century. The originals are pictured in Gareth Williams, *Master Pieces*, page 52. The woods used for these copies are yellow carabeen and forest sheoak.

Samuel Reiss opened the Grand Cigar Divan in The Strand in central London in 1828. The site had formerly been occupied by the Fountain Tavern, home of the Kit Kat Club. This club had been founded in the early eighteenth century by leading Whigs and the bookseller Jacob Tonson. Its first meetings were held in the house of Christopher Cat, hence the club's name. A literary and social club, it is chiefly remembered because portraits of its members were painted by Sir Godfrey Kneller.

The Divan soon developed as a coffee house where gentlemen smoked cigars with their coffee, browsed journals and newspapers, conversed, and played chess while sitting on the comfortable divans.

(A divan was originally a Turkish court of justice. Its meaning widened to include a council chamber, a reception room, a coffee-house, and a cushioned seat standing against the wall of a room). Regulars paid one guinea a year for coffee and use of the Divan. The daily entrance fee for others was 6d, or 1/6d with coffee and a cigar. Chess matches were sometimes played against other London coffee houses using top-hatted runners to carry the details of the moves.

In 1848 caterer John Simpson joined Samuel Reiss, the building was enlarged, and the focus shifted to food. Ree's Divan took over as London's leading center for chess.[24]

Today Simpson's-in-the-Strand is perhaps London's most famous "British" restaurant specialising in roast beef, and there is still one of the original Jaques Grand Cigar Divan chess sets if you want to have a game. Simpson's present dining room was the Divan Chess Salon.

Horae Divanianae, a collection of the early games played at the Divan was published in 1852 by E. Williams.[25]

Figure 1.51   One of the 62 of 65 pages which survived from the Jaques Pattern Book of 1795 to 1870 after the John Jaques & Son premises were bombed in the London Blitz of 1941. The sets shown on this page are *left*, old-English; and *right*, the Dublin pattern. Other pages from the same catalog are shown in the next four figures.

Courtesy of John Jaques and Son Limited.

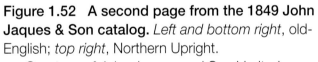

Figure 1.52   A second page from the 1849 John Jaques & Son catalog. *Left and bottom right*, old-English; *top right*, Northern Upright.
Courtesy of John Jaques and Son Limited.

Figure 1.53   Barleycorn sets pictured on a third page from the 1849 John Jaques & Son catalog.
Courtesy of John Jaques and Son Limited.

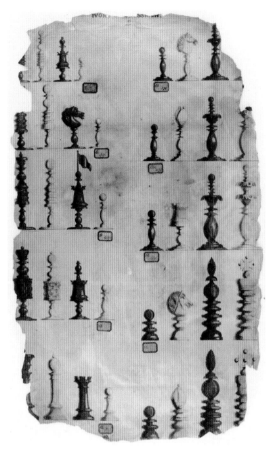

Figure 1.54   A fourth page from the 1849 John Jaques & Son catalog. *Top left*, barleycorn; *bottom left*, Northern Upright; *top right*, Calvert-style (a recent appellation); *bottom right*, St. George.

Courtesy of John Jaques and Son Limited.

Figure 1.55   Chess men, checkers, dominoes, and other games equipment pictured in the 1849 John Jaques & Son catalog.

The company was founded by Thomas Jaques, like your author of Huguenot descent. Thomas trained as a bone and ivory turner under a Mr Ivy in Holborn, London. He married Mr Ivy's niece, and on Mr Ivy's death in 1795 took over the business, renaming it "Thomas Jaques, (Manufacturer of Ivory, Hardwoods, Bone, and Tunbridge ware)".

Thomas's son John joined the firm, as did John's son John II. John II invented and the firm manufactured Happy Families, Tiddley-Winks, Ludo, and Snakes and Ladders, and introduced croquet into England from Ireland.

John Jaques III joined the family firm in 1894, and shortly afterwards invented what we now call table tennis. Originally called Gossima, it did not catch on until relaunched as Ping-Pong.

John Jaques and Son Limited is still run by Jaques family members, but is now in Thornton Heath, Surrey. It still makes a huge range of games equipment, and of course Staunton chessmen.[26]

Courtesy of John Jaques and Son Limited.

1.8 NORTH AMERICA

According to Fiske in *Chess in Iceland*, "In New England chess was almost unpractised until a century and a half (or more) after the country's settlement. To the colonists, therefore, the chess-board (or 'checker-board', as it was oftenest styled) was only known as a board used in the playing the game of draughts [checkers] . . . with little thought or knowledge of chess." By the early eighteenth century, however, chess was popular among the educated, and George Washington (1732–1799), Benjamin Franklin (1706–1790), Thomas Jefferson (1743–1826), and John Bartram (1699–1777) the "father of American botany" were keen chess players. Their sets, which were manufactured in Europe, survive,[27] but North American craftsmen would have been making replacement men and occasionally sets based on European designs by late in the eighteenth century. In the nineteenth, it was fittingly a citizen of the New World who invented a new approach to chess set design.

In 1864 architect Frederick. S. Copley introduced a chess set in which all its pieces communicated how they could be moved directly to players (figures 1.56 and 1.57). So revolutionary was this concept that it would be another sixty years before it was revisited.

AMERICAN CHESS WRITINGS AND CLUBS

Benjamin Franklin's "The Morals of Chess" was the first chess writing published in America; it appeared in 1786 in the *Columbian* magazine. The first American textbook on chess was published in Philadelphia in 1802; *Chess Made Easy* was essentially a reprint of the 1796 London edition of Philidor; it also contained Franklin's 1786 article.[28] The first chess manual written by an American, *The Elements of Chess*, was published in Boston in 1805. Its anonymous editor, William Blagrove, proposed that American chess pieces should have more appropriate names: for example, kings should be governors, queens should be generals, and pawns should be pioneers.[29]

A New York Chess Club was founded in 1801, and chess was played at the Athenaeum in Philadelphia from 1813.[30] North America was later to produce many master players, most notably Paul Morphy (1837–1884), Frank Marshall (1877–1944), and Bobby Fisher (1943–), world champion (1972– 1975).

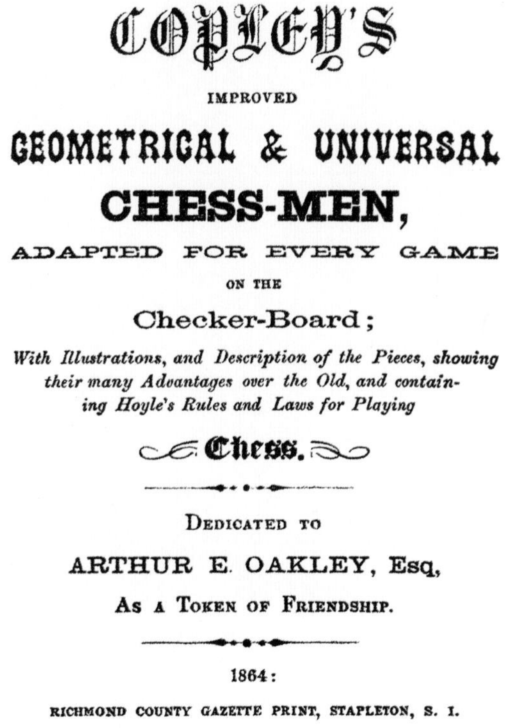

COPLEY'S

IMPROVED

GEOMETRICAL & UNIVERSAL CHESS-MEN,

ADAPTED FOR EVERY GAME

ON THE

Checker-Board;

With Illustrations, and Description of the Pieces, showing their many Advantages over the Old, and containing Hoyle's Rules and Laws for Playing

Chess.

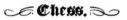

DEDICATED TO

ARTHUR E. OAKLEY, Esq,

AS A TOKEN OF FRIENDSHIP.

1864:

RICHMOND COUNTY GAZETTE PRINT, STAPLETON, S. I.

Figure 1.56 The title page of Copley's twelve-page pamphlet of 1864. The page size is only $4^{3}/_{4}$ in. x $3^{3}/_{8}$ in. (12 x 8.5 cm). In his pamphlet Copley explained the benefits of his "Improved Geometrical and Universal Chess-men" thus:

1. One set of men could be used for chess, draughts (checkers), backgammon, and a new game introduced by Copley called Chesica which was a hybrid of chess and draughts. Because the queen, bishop, knight, and rook chess pieces each consisted of a stack of two counters, there were 46 counters in a set for the four games.
2. The counters used were cheaper and more durable than conventional chessmen.
3. The designs of the pieces (see next figure) made chess easier to learn because their forms "indicate the direction in which they move at a glance".

Copley's use of "at a glance" suggests that he believed that players would perceive how to move any of his pieces more readily than they would conventional chess pieces.

A king counter is also a king piece. Its round shape represents its ability to move "all round" (in any direction).

A queen counter. As with the king, the queen counter's round shape represents its ability to move in any direction.

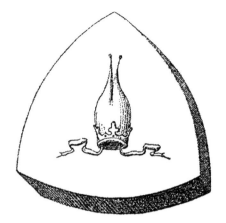

A bishop counter. Its triangular shape represents its diagonal movements.

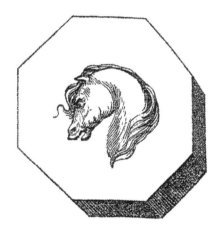

A knight counter. Its eight sides represent the eight squares which a knight can move onto if they are unoccupied.

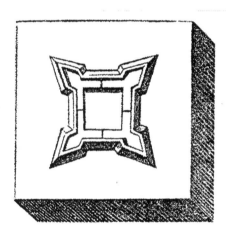

A rook counter. Its square form represents that it may move only along a rank or a file. The image is the plan of a fort in the style of Sébastien Le Prestre de Vauban (1653–1707).

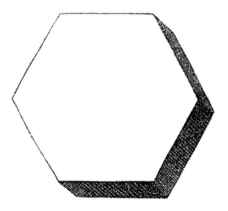

A pawn counter. Its hexagonal form has "three sides ranging forward (in the direction of their move)" indicating the three directions of movement. Copley's pawn counter is also used singly as a piece because, except for its first move, it can only move one square—as explained below, the other pieces are each formed by a stack of two counters.

Figure 1.57 Copley's six counter designs. Copley designed his pieces' forms to show beginners how they moved. Because the queen, bishop, knight, and rook can move more than one square at a time, two identical counters of the appropriate type were stacked like kings in checkers (draughts in Britain) to represent the chess pieces. The representative symbols on the counters are therefore redundant. No Copley counters have survived.

Illustrations for this and figure 1.56 courtesy of John G. White Chess and Checkers Collection, Cleveland Public Library, Ohio. Its pamphlet was copied from the only-known original in the Library of Congress, Washington D.C.

1.9 THE TWENTIETH CENTURY

ART AND DESIGN

The Industrial Revolution dominated the nineteenth century in much of Europe and in North America, and was in turn often accompanied by the degradation and enslavement of factory workers, and an excess of machine-made ornament which became all too apparent in the 1851 Great Exhibition in London.

The Arts and Crafts solution of a return to medieval means of production was superficially attractive, but even ardent supporter William Morris had been unable to show through his company Morris and Co. that it was realistic other than for luxury goods. Others had a different vision for a better future: through government intervention the lot of the worker at work could be improved, while through the greater and cheaper production of better-designed goods, living conditions outside work could be raised, and workers and their families would be enabled to seek artistic and intellectual fulfillment and become full members of society.

Implicit in this new vision of designing was the rationalization of applied ornament and decoration. Calls for this were not new, but they were reinforced from an unexpected quarter, primitive art—its simple forms and bold colors were both aesthetically powerful (figure 1.58), and could be compatible with manufacturing. Primitive art was also influential in promoting the revolt against accurate, detailed imitation in art which the avant-garde had come to regard as exhausted and theoretically bereft. This revolt left a design vacuum which was filled by a succession of "isms"—there are at least a dozen of them, starting with cubism and futurism. These isms reflected the increasing presence of science and theory in life, and therefore in art.

CHESSMEN

Throughout the twentieth century Staunton sets made by Jaques (figure 1.59), and the numerous and usually inferior versions made by other manufacturers, were by far the biggest sellers in the West. This conservatism was not restricted to chess set buyers—the majority

Figure 1.58 Sophisticated primitive art, a carved, wooden set from the 1930s. The name of its designer/ maker is not known. The king is 4³/4 in. (121 mm) tall.
Polumbaum Collection. Photographs by Risa Korris.

of craftspeople who made chess sets copied established designs (figure 1.60). But copying was not universal; chess set design also attracted avant-garde artists and designers.

An early and important art ism for chess set design was dada. It was "anarchic, nihilistic, and disruptive [and] . . . denied the value of [conventional] art.[31] A leading dadaist was Marcel Duchamp (1887–1968) who introduced and started exhibiting his *ready-mades* in 1915 in New York. By selecting an everyday manufactured object as a work of art, Duchamp defined it as a work of art. This approach lead to chess sets being made by others directly from machine-made components originally made for other purposes (figure 1.61).

Duchamp abandoned art for chess when he returned to France from America in 1923, and was good enough to enter the first world amateur chess championship in 1924.[32] He continued to play in major chess tournaments for another decade.

Duchamp seems to have designed little chess equipment—one travelling set, and a suite consisting of a table and chess set (figure 1.62).[33] His major contribution was to stimulate and maintain an interest in chess and chessmen among other avant-garde artists.

The ism which followed dada was surrealism, which supposedly involved the recording of dreams. Three of its titans, Man Ray, Yves Tanguy, and Max Ernst designed chess sets (figures 1.63 to 1.65) which, however, cannot be classified as surrealist—the three obviously accepted the importance of playability, and at least one (Man Ray) desired that his designs would be mass produced (they weren't).

The sets by Duchamp, Ray, Tanguy, Ernst and other major avant-garde artists inspired less well-known artists (figure 1.66). The new product design professionals were also attracted to the medium. Both groups sought clever and original ways to exploit concepts such as:

1. Overt mathematical and geometric nicety and playfullness. An extension of this was the property of nesting or fitting nicely into a box or other container—the chess sets designed by Hartwig at the Bauhaus were among the earliest manifestations of this approach (figure 1.67). A later example was the set designed by Cy Enfield in 1972 which fitted onto a perspex rod.[34]

2. The apparent modernity and sympathy with the

Figure 1.59 A mid-twentieth-century Staunton set by Jaques. The knights heads have lost their nineteenth-century vigor. These white men are boxwood, the black men are ebony.
Photographed courtesy of Mr and Mrs John Powell.

machine age aesthetic of Phileban forms (created by rotating shapes composed of circular arcs and straight lines about an axis).

3. Using chess sets to promote beliefs, typically those concerned with politics, human rights, and the environment. Yoko Ono (born 1933), for example, exhibited the first version of the chess set Play it by Trust at the Indica Gallery, London, in 1966. The men were commercial Staunton-style, but all (and the board) were painted white. Ono's concept was that during play the players would forget which sides the men belonged to, come to see themselves not at war or in conflict, and thus be freed to develop a new relationship based on empathy.[35]

4. Differentiation of pieces based not on representative form and decoration, but on hitherto unexploited properties such as weight or smell. The designing of sets whose pieces communicated "directly" how they should be moved, initiated by Copley in the nineteenth century, was much explored in the twentieth.

5. Duchamp's ready-mades. Small commercial containers for cosmetics, drinks, cleaning products were trialed, but were not convincing.

6. The guest designer. A chess set designed by a notable in the arts, popular music, television, film, etc. was likely to be more marketable. Ringo Starr was for example the joint designer of a chess set in silver for Asprey & Co., London, in 1972. Each piece was a hand with different finger and thumb positions, and with a different cuff or glove.[36]

7. Themes based not on medieval society, which had been contemporary when introduced, but on for example: more recent historical events; the contemporary media, especially on TV shows, and films, and popular books; science fiction; and physical, including sexual, characteristics. An example of the last is a set based on hands by Gene Zelazny. It differs from the Ringo Starr set by using the thumb and finger positions of deaf-mute sign language to signify the pieces.[37]

The introduction of new designs was aided by developments in materials, particularly plastics and resins, and manufacturing processes. In 1891 The British Chess Company was marketing Xylonite chessmen,[38] and Jaques was manufacturing Celluloid

chessmen in the 1920s.[39] (Paradoxically the ease and cheapness of molding and casting plastics and resins enabled figurative sets to be produced almost as cheaply as non-figurative, but not until the last quarter of the twentieth century did this catalyze design innovation in mass-produced sets. However because playability was often not a primary consideration for some designers, the dominance of the Staunton and other earlier playing chess set designs continued.

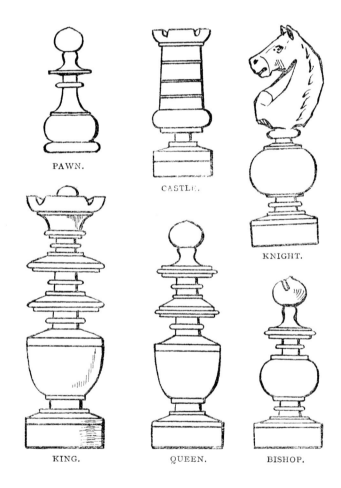

Figure 1.60 Conservatism in chess set design. British woodworkers in the 1930s were not encouraged to create new designs; they were expected to copy established nineteenth-century sets. This version of the Regency design was promoted in the instructional book *Wood-Turning* (London: Evans Brothers), page 135. Similar pieces are shown in figure 1.32 of this book.

Figure 1.61 Not ready-made chess pieces because I have creatively selected and assembled the fasteners. The essense of the true ready-made is that the artist does not input any of his or her own creativity. These pieces do however illustrate that art can be created from mundane objects which would conventionally be considered antithetical to art.

To distinguish the sides I could use paint or plating. Similar sets are shown in F. Lanier Graham, *Chess Sets*, pages 58 and 59, and Colleen Schafroth, *The Art of Chess*, page 152.

Figure 1.62 Copies of the king, rook, and pawn of a set designed by Marcel Duchamp in 1919 in Buenos Aires. The copy of the rook is in spotted gum, the king, queen and pawn are in spalted plum.

The set's design is perhaps derived from the Staunton, but although the knights (not shown) imitate a horse's head and neck, they are carved in a distinctly non-European style and have a metal base.

The square top and placement of the embrasures strongly symbolize the rook's movements along the files and ranks, perhaps the first instance since Frederick Copley's counters shown in figure 1.57. Square-towered rooks had been used before, but they lack the overt directional quality of Duchamp's form, see Hans and Siegfried Wichmann, *Chess*, plates 114, 116, and 117.

An illustration of Duchamp's full set appears in the 2003 booklet *The Art of Chess*, page 6. Pages 22 and 23 show the set on its a chess table, and a travelling set, both designed by Duchamp.

Figure 1.63   A 1944 variation by Man Ray on his original 1920 design. Made in 1945, it features fresh symbols, and an absense of fussy detail.

1. The king is a pyramid, associated with the kings (pharoahs) of Egypt, albeit with their lives after death.
2. The queen imitates a medieval lady's headdress.
3. The bishop imitates a bishop's miter.
4. The knight could be a stylized imitation of a horse's head and neck; it also suggests the piece's "diagonal" movement.
5. The rook imitates a tower. The two channels imitate embrasures, and together with the square plan-shape of the piece, indicate the rook's movements along the ranks and files.
6. The pawn is a pared-down traditional design. It also resembles an Algerian style of pawn, but whether Ray was aware of it is unknown.

Man Ray (1890–1976) was born in Philadelphia, and became an important painter, sculptor, photographer, and filmmaker. He is particularly associated with dada and surrealism. He met Marcel Duchamp in 1915, and they often played together thereafter. In about 1920 Ray designed his first chess set which was a modified Staunton. The prototype was made using items lying about in his studio. Three copies were made in silver in 1926, one for the Maharajah of Indore.[40]

Ray continued to design variations on his original set until about 1962, and limited numbers of the variations were made in wood and aluminum.[41] The later the set, the more customary the piece symbols tended to be. He also designed a chess table in 1930, and a chess board in 1962.[42]

Courtesy Philadelphia Museum of Art: Gift of John F. Harbeson.

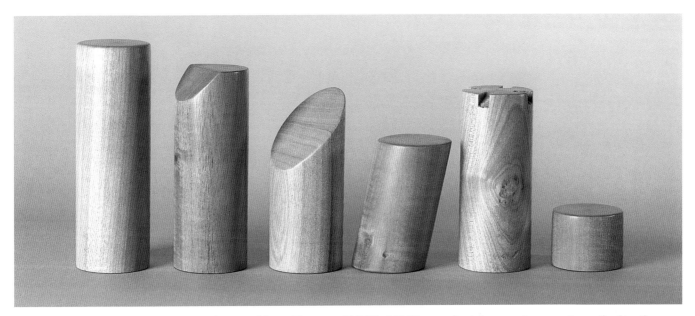

Figure 1.64   Pieces based on the set Yves Tanguy (1900–1955) created from a broom handle for the 1944 New York exhibition The Imagery of Chess organized by Man Ray. Tanguy's piece forms are based on the cylinder, and are differentiated by flat cut surfaces and their heights. In Paris in 1927 Tanguy found his unique surrealist painting style. He moved to the United States in 1939.

Figure 1.65   Max Ernst's 1944 set owes much to primitive art, and is perhaps the best known design of the twentieth century. Apart from a vague similarity in style and the presence of the cone, there are no features common to all pieces.

The form of the king, second from the right, gives no clue as to what piece it is, and conflicts with that of Tanguy's bishop (figure 1.64). Ernst's king is also shorter than his queen, is the reverse of what is customary, but reflects the relative attacking power of the two pieces.

Born in Germany in 1891, Ernst became a convert to dada, and moved to Paris in 1922 where he then became a prominent surrealist artist. Ernst moved to United States in 1939, returned to Paris in 1949, and died there in 1976.

Courtesy Philadelphia Museum of Art: Gift of John F. Harbeson.

Figure 1.66   Big Sur by Franz Sundow, California, 1951, turned and carved boxwood. The king is 4^5/8 in. (116 mm) tall. The king and queen are poorly differentiated.

    The early-nineteenth-century board is 14 in. (356 mm) square, and made in pine and walnut.

    Courtesy Philadelphia Museum of Art: Gift of John F. Harbeson.

Figure 1.67 Bauhaus set designed by Josef Hartwig (1880–1956), and first manufactured in 1924 in unstained and stained pear wood.. Hartwig was appointed leader of the wood carving and sculpture workshop at the Bauhaus in 1921. Other versions were made in 1922 and 1924, and replicas have been manufactured more recently.[43]

Copley's counters (figure 1.57) first manifested the idea that each piece's form could represent its movements, but it does not seem to have been known in Europe in the 1920s. Instead Hartwig's design seems to have stemmed from an idea of the De Stijl artist Vilmos Huszar. The difference in form between the king and queen does not demonstrate that the king can only move one square whereas the queen is permitted to move any available distance difference. The Bauhaus men are also designed to pack neatly. The label was designed by Joost Schmidt.

This set was owned by Walter Gropius (1883–1969), first director of the Bauhaus from its commencement in 1919 in Weimar, Germany, until 1928. Gropius invented the school's name from the German verb *bauen* meaning "building" and *haus* meaning house. Gropius was also conscious that it resembled the word Bauhutte, the name of the medieval guild of builders and stonemasons, and therefore reflected the concept of common effort. In 1925 the Bauhaus moved to Dessau. In 1932 it moved to Berlin. It closed in 1933.

Polumbaum Collection. Photographs by Risa Korris.

1.10 THE TWENTY-FIRST CENTURY

The media profile of chess in the West has declined since the retirement of Bobby Fisher from tournaments in 1975. Yet, despite the increasing competition for leisure time, chess remains enormously popular and is played, even if only occasionally, by several hundred million people. There must be billions of extant chessmen.

During the second half of the twentieth century and since there have been changes which have affected the designing, making, and prices of chess sets:

1. Mass production of playing sets has moved to lower labor cost countries, particular India and China (figure 1.68). You can now buy a reasonable quality wooden Staunton-style sets very cheaply. Plastic, resin, and glass sets are often similarly priced. These sets have undermined the market both for wooden sets made by Western companies, and by self-employed Western craftspeople.
2. There is a growing shortage of elephant ivory. Its trade is now curtailed by international agreement to protect the remaining elephants. Whale jaw bone is similarly difficult to obtain. Artificial ivories and other synthetic compounds can be used instead, but lack the appeal.

3. The supply of the woods such as box, ebony, and African blackwood traditionally preferred for high-quality chessmen is decreasing. Their costs are therefore increasing.
4. Artists have been unable to generate any major new isms in recent decades, and have lapsed into recycling earlier ones.

These changes are not the deathknell for those who would make chess sets, they are merely restraints and challenges to be overcome. And there are positives:

1. The introduction of electronic chess boards and computer chess has not rendered "conventional" chess equipment undesirable because the latter's aesthetic appeal remains greater.
2. There is greater interest in collecting chess sets than ever before, and more people can afford to buy expensive sets if they want to. However collectors still focus on sets made in earlier centuries.

There is therefore infinite scope to design new chess sets, both for conventional use on a horizontal board, and for use in new situations. A recent example of the latter is the invention of fridge-magnet chessmen by Britons Marty Fox and Scott Stirling.

Figure 1.68   A turned, painted set of apparently Eastern European design made in Taiwan in the 1990s, and retailed very cheaply. The figurative forms are assembled from turned components.

1.11 ENDNOTES

1. Harold James Ruthven Murray (1868–1955) was the eldest of six sons of James and Ada Murray (there were also five daughters). James Murray was editor of the *Oxford English Dictionary* from 1879 to his death in 1915. The publication of the first edition of the OED was completed in 1928. Harold's book was also, and continues to be, published by Oxford University Press.

2. The seven men are now in the collection of the Uzbekistan State Museum for Preserving the History of Culture and Art in Samarkand. They were made in the seventh or eight century, are carved in ivory, and are between 1 and 1.6 in. (26 and 41 mm) tall. The king is a shah holding a mace, seated on a throne on a carriage pulled by three horses. The queen is a farzin mounted on a horse, accompanied by a mounted rider. The bishop (pil) is a war elephant ridden by a soldier. The knight (asp) has a shield and sword, and is mounted on a horse. The rook (ruhk) is a chariot pulled by three horses. The two pawns (pujadas) each hold a shield and a sword. The best accessible photographs are in I. M. Linder, *The Art of Chess Pieces*, pp. 60–63. The men are also pictured in Gareth Williams, *Master Pieces*, pp. 14–15, but he believes that the rook is a knight.

3. Barbara Brend, *Islamic Art* (London: British Museum Press, 1991), p. 17.

4. Hadiths are well explained in Trevor Mostyn and Albert Hourani, editors, *The Cambridge Encyclopedia of the Middle East and North Africa* (Cambridge University Press, 1988), pp. 161–162.

5. Robert Irwin, *Islamic Art* (London: Laurence King Publishing, 1997), p. 80.

6. At least three books (by Finkel, Stratford, and Taylor) have been published about the Lewis chessmen; they are listed in this book's bibliography. Other references include: Gareth Williams, "Book Review of The Lewis Chessmen by Neil Stratford," *The Chess Collector* (July 1977): p. 22; and Bird, "The Lewis Chessmen and the Meristems of Murram Grass," *The Chess Collector* (July 1996).

7. During the early medieval period the main source of ivory for European carvers was walrus tusks, see Daniel J. Boorstin, *The Discoverers* (London: J. M. Dent, 1984), p. 215.

8. Hans and Siegfried Wichmann, *Chess*, p. 29.

9. Richard Eales, *Chess: The History of a Game*, pp. 50–51.

10. Prof. Ned Munger, "Afghans vs. Sikhs Chess Set," *The Chess Collector* (Spring 2002): pp. 3–6.

11. An excellent source for information on Caxton is Richard Deacon, *William Caxton* (London: Frederick Muller), 1976.

12. H. J. R. Murray, *A History of Chess*, p. 769.

13. Dr. Victor Keats, "Thomas Hyde's Book of Oriental Games," *The Chess Collector* (Summer–Autumn 2001): pp. 3–5.

14. J. C. Drummond and Anne Wilbraham, *The Englishman's Food* (London: Pimlico, 1991), p. 116.

15. The Café de la Régence was opened in 1670 by an American, but did not become a chess venue until about 1740. It relocated in 1755. Its chess room was closed in 1916. The full story of the Café de la Régence is told in Ken Whyld, *Café de la Régence* (Caistor, Lincolnshire, 1953).

16. Maguelonne Toussaint-Samat, *History of Food* (Oxford: Blackwell Publishers, 1994), p. 587.

17. Slaughters was not just a venue for chess, it was also the home of "a society of literary and scientific men" which included botanists Joseph Banks and Daniel Solander, potters Josiah Wedgwood and Thomas Bentley, and industrialist Matthew Boulton; see Jenny Uglow, *The Lunar Men* (London: Faber and Faber, 2002), p.125.

18. Quoted in Richard Eales, *Chess the History of a Game*, p. 117. Eales states that the quotation is taken from Richard Twiss, *Chess*, vol. I 1787, vol.II 1789.

19. H. J. R. Murray, *A History of Chess*, p. 191. For a discussion of blindfold chess, see David Hooper and Kenneth Whyld, *The Oxford Companion to Chess*, pp. 36–37.

20. The first public railway, between Stockton and Darlington in England, opened on September 27th, 1825. The Liverpool to Manchester railway opened in 1830, and the line from London to Birmingham in 1838. The first railways opened in France in 1832, and in Germany in 1835. The first commercial railway in America between Baltimore and Ellicott's Mills was 13 miles (21 km) long and opened in 1830.

21. Readers wishing to follow the evidence and differences in opinion regarding the genesis of the Staunton design might start with: Michael Mark, *British Chess Sets*; Michael Mark "Nathaniel Cook(e) and the Staunton Chessman," *The Chess Collector* (Spring 2003): pp.3–6; Barry Martin "Enigma Variations-Cooking the Facts," *The Chess Collector* (Summer 2003): p. 3; and Robert E. Stoller "Reflections on the Staunton Design," enclosed in *The Chess Collector* (Autumn–Winter 2002, Spring 2003, and Summer 2003).

22. David Hooper and Kenneth Whyld, *The Oxford Companion to Chess*, p. 374. Donald M. Liddell, *Chessmen*, p. 94, gives the founding year as 1849.

23. Michael Mark, *British Chess Sets*, set 24.

24. Donald M. Liddell, *Chessmen*, p. 94.

25. Donald M. Liddell, *Chessmen*, p. 94.

26. *John Jaques 1795–1995* (Thornton Heath: John Jaques and Son Limited, 1995).

27. Gareth Williams' *Master Pieces* shows sets similar to George Washington's and Benjamin Franklin's on pages 38 to 39 and 40 to 41 respectively. Chapter VI on pages 42 to 51 of Donald M. Liddell, *Chessmen*, is titled "Famous Owners and Designers of Chessmen", and shows Franklin's, Washington's, and Bertram's sets.

28. Fred Wilson, *A Picture History of Chess*, p. 18; also Gareth Williams, *Master Pieces*, p. 38.

29. Fred Wilson, *A Picture History of Chess*, p. 18.

30. Donald M. Liddell, *Chessmen*, p. 95.

31. Hugh Honour and John Fleming, *A World History of Art*, 5th ed (London: Lawrence King, 1999), p. 802.

32. Dawn Ades, Neil Cox, and David Hopkins, *Marcel Duchamp* (London: Thames and Hudson, 1999), p. 140.

33. *The Art of Chess* (London: Somerset House, Gilbert Collection, 2003). Published in conjunction with the exhibition of chess sets titled "The Art of Chess".

34. Harold Newman, *An Illustrated Dictionary of Silverware* (London: Thames and Hudson, 1987), p. 72.

35. *The Art of Chess* (London: Somerset House, Gilbert Collection, 2003).

36. Harold Newman, *An Illustrated Dictionary of Silverware*, pp. 71–72.

37. *The Chess Collector* (Spring 2000): p. 7.

38. Robert E. Stoller "Reflections on the Staunton Design," p. 6; enclosure in *The Chess Collector* (Spring 2003). English chemist Alexander Parkes developed the first plastic in 1862 by softening nitrocellulose with vegetable oils and camphor. He called it Parkesine, and it was used as a substitute for ivory and tortoiseshell. It was later called Xylonite. From 1869 it was called Celluloid in the United States.

39. *The Chess Collector* (Summer–Autumn 2001): p 16.

40. Michael Mark "Man Ray at Sotheby's" *The Chess Collector* 4, no. 2: pp. 5–11.

41. F. Lanier Graham, *Chess Sets*, p. 66; Arturo Schwartz, *Man Ray* (London: Thames and Hudson, 1977), pp. 203–205, and plates 325–328; and Gareth Williams, *Master Pieces*, pp. 132–133.

42. Man Ray was alert to the commercial potential for chess sets, and in 1919 consulted American chessmaster Frank Marshall who seems to have been ambivalent. Ray also consulted the world chess champion, Alexander Alekhine, who agreed to allow his name to be used to promote Ray's designs. Because of the uncertainty of success and the financial investment required, Ray decided to continue to produce his sets only in small numbers as art works.

43. Jeannine Fiedler and Peter Feierabend, editors, *Bauhaus* (Cologne: Könemann, 1999), pp. 406, 416–417, 633.

Chapter Two

GALLERY

This chapter shows sets made recently by just six woodturners. There are many other turners who have made sets which merit inclusion. Perhaps I should do a book titled 200 *Contemporary Turned Chess Sets*.

The sets illustrated demonstrate different intentions and different styles. The sets also illustrate that there remains unlimited potential for design innovation even within an area of functional turning which is at least a thousand years old.

Copyright is only waived for the designs by Mike Darlow and Len Clarke

2.1 STEVEN ADDAMS

Figures 2.1 to 2.9 show a chess set and table by Steven Addams of Salem, Oregon, USA. In 1996 Steven began to play chess with friends, and having an arts and crafts background, soon determined to make his own chess equipment despite never having turned.

He first developed the detailed design drawings (figure 2.3). He then bought a Klein lathe, and worked on the table and men during 1997 and 1998. What particularly impresses are the care, thought, attention to detail, and the willingness to commit 2000 hours of evenings and weekends.

The black men are made from African blackwood, *Dalbergia melanoxylon*. Although one of the densest and hardest woods, because it is a true rosewood (of the genus *Dalbergia*), it carves better than any of the ebonies which belong to the genus *Diospyros*. The white men are made from ivory.

Ivory tusk has a vein hole of between 0.5 and 1.5 mm diameter running through its center. Steven often affixed scrap wood with hot-melt glue to aid sawing the tusk economically into vein-free blanks. For turning, the ivory and blackwood blanks were super-glued to pieces of scrap wood which were in turn screwed onto faceplates.

Both ivory and blackwood scrape superbly, and for this Steven made his own tools from HSS twist drills

(figure 2.5). The turning was done between centers with a live tail center. All the men except the knights were turned in one piece.

Figure 2.1   A chess table by Steven Addams.
The board has a cover of figured bubinga with thirty-two leather pockets to store the men when not in use. The board is 27 in. (690 mm) square, and 1$^{1}/_{4}$ in. (32 mm) thick; its underside is covered with suede leather, and the legs are removable.

Figure 2.2 The Addams board.

The border is book-matched, solid, fiddleback maple with cocobolo inlays.

The parking recesses for captured men are a novel feature. The recesses hold disks of blackwood or of ivory. Each disk has a bevelled top edge bordered with a circle of copper-plated lead strip similar to the came (H-sectioned lead strip) used in stained-glass windows.

The squares have bevelled edges and are cut from two types of marble. Bevelled diamonds in ivory are fitted between the corners of the squares of ranks 1 and 2; the diamonds between ranks 7 and 8 are of blackwood (see the central drawing in figure 2.3). The squares and diamonds are surrounded by came in the same way as the disks in the parking recesses.

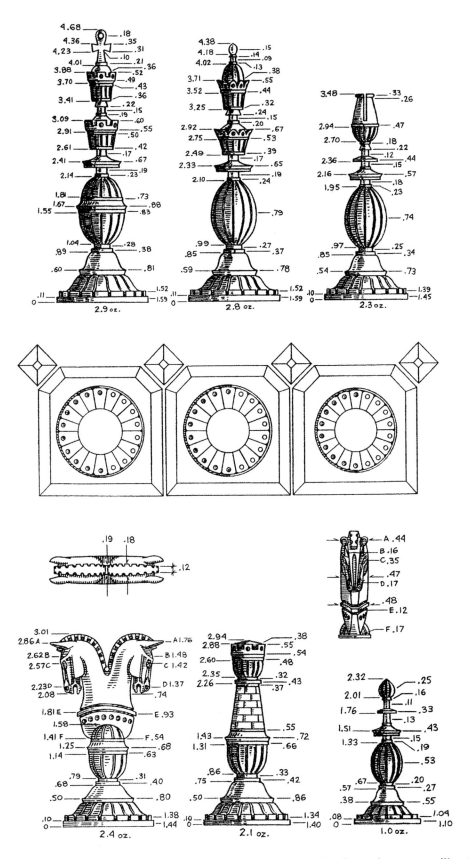

Figure 2.3 Steven Addams' detailed drawings of the pieces and the board squares illustrate the care he took with the project.

Figure 2.4   The six white pieces of the Addams chess set in African elephant ivory. Steven was able to buy the ivory legally because it was already in America before the ban on international ivory trading was introduced. The king is 4⁵/₈ in. (119 mm) tall.

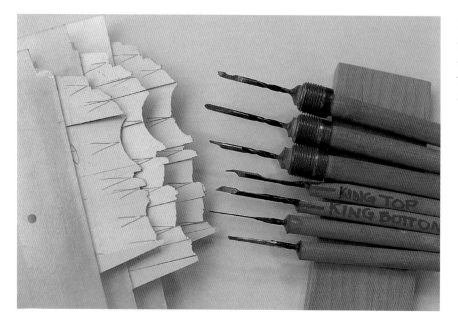

Figure 2.5   Scraping turning tools ground by Steven from HSS twist drills. The three plastic templates are for the bishop (*front*), king, and queen, and are shown upside down.

Figure 2.6 **Fluting with a rotating burr driven via a flexible shaft.** The bearing at the end of the flexible rotating shaft is screwed to a horizontal steel disk which can be moved about on the level wooden surface to follow the surface of a chessman.

The dividing plate and index at the left-hand end of the headstock were used to rotate the workpiece in increments of 30°, and lock the workpiece after each 30° rotation.

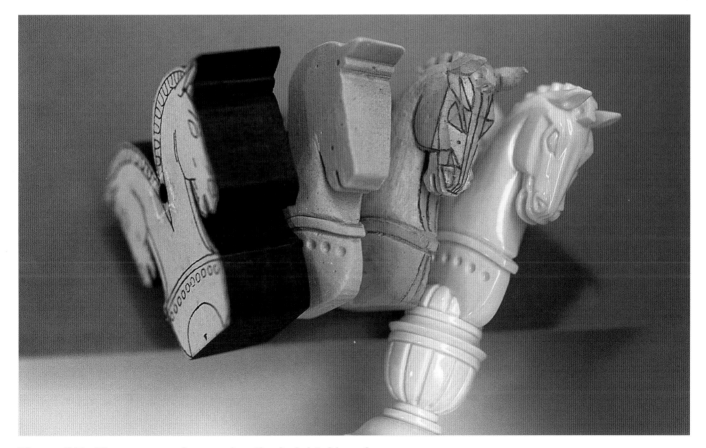

Figure 2.7 **The process for carving the knights' heads.**
About ten prototypes were cast and carved from automotive body filler before the design and procedure were finalized. Both hand carving tools and rotating burrs were used.

Figure 2.8 A black knight. The high gloss results from hours of fine sanding followed by an airbrushed coat of clear automobile polyurethane.

Figure 2.9 Covering and branding the bottoms of chessmen.

Left, a nonelectric branding iron "carved" from a $3/4$ in. (19 mm) diameter brass rod. The design combines an *A* for Addams with a king's head.

Right, the bottom of a white chessman covered with a branded leather disk. Darker-colored leather was used for the disks under the black men. The disk covers a cavity containing not lead but tungsten, which is 1.7 times denser than lead, and readily available from golf club component supply companies. A third of the required tungsten powder was mixed to a mortar with superglue and the catalyst hardener in the cavity in the man, then quickly stirred: this was repeated twice more. The bottom was then sanded flat before the leather disk was attached with double-stick tape.

2.2   MICHAEL BROLLY

Figure 2.10   Chess Set, 2001, by Michael J. Brolly of Mertztown, Pennsylvania. The pawns are turned on three axes, the other pieces on one. Michael turned the top halves of the heads of the queens and bishops separately, then glued them onto the bottom halves of the heads (which are integral with their bodies) with eye disks between. Vertical segments of the heads are cut away to reveal the eyes.

The woods are holly and bubinga. The kings are 7 in. (178 mm) tall.

The 20 x 20 in. (508 x 508 mm) glass board is by Ted Cooper.

2.3 LEN CLARKE

Len Clarke of Cheltenham, England, designed and made the chessmen in figure 2.11 for his grandchildren, but I'm sure that adults would enjoy the men just as much as children. The men can also double as toy figures for play outside chess.

Len's use of bold turnings, both alone and with added simple components, a limited range of different woods, some drilling, and simple painting is won-derfully effective, and opens the door to a host of figurative design possibilities.

The white men are in sycamore, the black are in pear. Differently colored paints and fabrics are also used to differentiate the sides. Other features recall differentiations used in the Charlemagne and other early chessmen: one side has fifteenth-century pointed shields, the other has circular shields; the pawns and bishops of the two sides have differently shaped miters and bodies; and the castle towers of the two sides differ in form.

Those familiar with chess history may find Len's elephant knights a little confusing, the elephant being first the bishop of chaturanga, and centuries later, with a houdah in the form of a castle tower, a rook. If you are inspired to design a set based on Len's, you might consider replacing his elephant with a creature more equine in form; for example, a fully turned horse's head similar to that in figure 1.68.

Figure 2.11 Len Clarke's medieval chess set. The kings are 7 in. (178 mm) tall, the pawns 4 in. (102 mm) tall. The pieces of the two sides alternate in the two photographs. Detailed drawings for these men are included in Len's article "Elephants and castles" *The Woodturner* (May/June 2003): pages 12 to 14.

2.4   MIKE DARLOW

I ran a large commercial woodturning firm for about twenty years. This probably influenced my choice of design intentions which have been to keep the turning durations low and minimize hand carving while retaining piece symbols which Western players would recognize. The design developments shown in figures 2.12 to 2.16 reflect the increases in my knowledge of the history of chess set design over twenty years.

I name my chess set designs after chess notables.

Figure 2.12   My first chess set made in about 1983 in silver ash and Queensland walnut when my knowledge of chess sets was then restricted to a familiarity with the Staunton design.

My piece designs are poorly integrated: the king is phallic, which has no connection to the other piece designs; the body of the queen is skirt-like; the bishop closely resembles that of Man Ray's in figure 1.63 (an example of parallel plagiarism); and the rook's form is more traditional than the others.

Figure 2.13   The Lopez design, named after Ruy López, author of the chess text *Libro de la invencion liberal y arte del juego del Axedrez*, published in Spain, in 1561.

This and the next set were made in 2000. The trigger was buying A. E. J. Mackett-Beeson's *Chessmen* and reading Harry Golombek's *Chess: A History*.

The bodies are forest sheoak, the tops are silver ash and Queensland walnut.

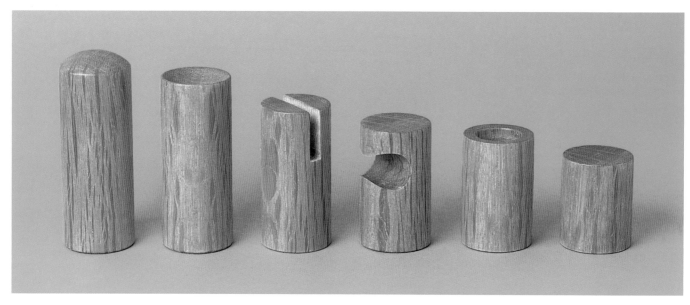

Figure 2.14   The Cessolis design. When I made this set I did not know of Yves Tanguy's broomstick set (figure 1.64). As with Tanguy's set, the ease of making is offset by the absence of easy-to-grip heads.

The domed head of the king mates with the recess of the same but opposite curvature in the top of the queen. The transverse drilling of the knight (done while the blank is still of square cross section) is based on a knight by Jorn Pfab, made in 1976, and pictured in *Arts and Crafts of Hamburg and Northern Germany*, Hyogo Prefectural Museum of Modern Art, 1985, exhibit 370.

The wood is forest sheoak.

Figure 2.15   The Stamma design. I originally christened this design "Philidor", not being aware of the nineteenth-century, commercial design of the same name. The bases are bulky to allow leading.

The wood is Tasmnian oak. The black side is stained green.

Figure 2.16 Caxton II, made in 2003 when this book was well advanced. A request to exhibit triggered a desire to design a set which combined the piece designs pictured in Caxton's woodcuts (figure 1.16) with the Staunton piece designs. The woods are Australian-grown English oak and Australian rose mahogany.

2.5 ERNIE NEWMAN

Figure 2.17 The white pieces from a set turned by Ernie Newman of Blaxland, New South Wales, but largely designed by his eleven-year-old son John Newman.

The king and queen resemble the same Staunton pieces. The bishop wears a bowler hat; the slot in the customary miter has been modified to create a smile. The knight peers through his helmet's visor. A cannon swivels atop the rook. When a pawn reaches the far rank and is promoted, it climbs aboard its own tank.

The wood is from an English oak planted in 1792 at Richmond, New South Wales. This tree was the first oak planted in Australia; it was killed by lightning in the 1980s. The black side (none of which is pictured) is in River Red Gum, the most widely dispersed Australian tree. The choice of woods alludes to the tension between the English colonizers and the aboriginal Australians.

2.6 REG HAWTHORNE

Reg Hawthorne of Gloucestershire, England, designed
and made the miniature chess set, board, and pawn-
shaped box shown in figures 2.18 and 2.19

The chessmen are in ebony and boxwood, and their
forms are based on those of the Staunton pieces. Their
heights are between $^{1}/_{2}$ and 1 in. (12 and 25 mm). The
box has three parts which screw together to give a total
height of $4^{1}/_{4}$ in. (108 mm).

The board is walnut with 64 holes drilled into its
top face. Short ebony and boxwood cinders were glued
into the holes to form the "squares".

This ensemble won the Society of Ornamental
Turners' Howe cup for plain turning in 2002.

Figure 2.18 The pawn box screwed together.

Figure 2.19 The box unscrewed to show how the men are stored within. *Left*, the bottom section of the
box holds the sixteen pawns in its outer annular channel, and the bishops and rooks in its deeper, inner
channel. *Center*, the kings, queens, and knights are stored within the box's center section.

Chapter Three

PIECE SYMBOLS

This chapter discusses chess piece symbols, and concentrates on those which can be turned and are customary in the West, such as kings' and queens' crowns, and rooks' castle towers.

When designing a piece symbol, you have to decide whether to

1. Imitate a person or thing, and if so to what accuracy.
2. Copy or adapt an earlier piece symbol instead of imitating the person or thing.
3. Stylize the person or thing or an earlier piece symbol. This is a sensible option where faithful imitation would demand a standard of artistry and workmanship which you cannot or do not wish to meet.
4. Select or design a fresh piece symbol; for example, the pyramid which Man Ray adopted for his kings (figure 1.63).

A piece symbol should not be designed in isolation, but should coherently relate to the others used in the set. My first set pictured in figure 2.12 disappoints because its piece symbols do not conform to any one schema. A second restraint is recognition—should the players who you would expect to use the set be able to readily recognize which pieces the symbols represent? This depends on which symbols are customary in that market. Particularly for carved or modelled sets, themes can be adopted which utilize non-customary piece signatures which may confuse

those playing with them for the first time. Relatedness and recognition are discussed in detail in chapter 4.

All piece symbols intended to resemble a person or thing are in one sense already stylized because the persons and things are reproduced at different scales. The castle tower is scaled down much more than a crown or miter because of the need to have all the chessmen in a set similar in size. Figure 3.1 illustrates this for two-dimensional symbols. The relative sizes of three-dimensional piece symbols may also be affected by

1. The status or importance of the originating person or thing—thus a miter is often imitated at a smaller scale than a king's crown.
2. The intention to reflect the chess pieces' relative powers. These ratios for modern pieces are queen, 9; rook 5; bishop and knight, 3; and pawn, 1. These ratios are however usually too extreme to exploit accurately.
3. Aesthetic considerations which illustrate Sir Ernst Gombrich's sense of order,[2] chiefly the intention that the piece heights, and often also the piece symbol heights, conform to some schema. This is discussed in the next chapter.
4. The need to better differentiate pieces.
5. Whether the form of a piece consists solely of a piece symbol, or a piece symbol and other parts and part-groups, such as a base or pedestal.

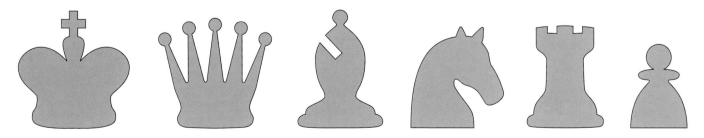

Figure 3.1 Today's customary, Western, two-dimensional piece symbols. The silhouettes for the two sides would typically be colored black and white or white and red.

Other factors which should influence the design of piece symbols include how they affect accessing and moving the pieces, stability, and durability.

3.1 KING PIECE SYMBOLS

Man Ray's adoption of a Pharaoh's pyramid as his king's piece symbol is a rare example of the usurpation of the crown as the king's piece symbol (figure 1.63). The

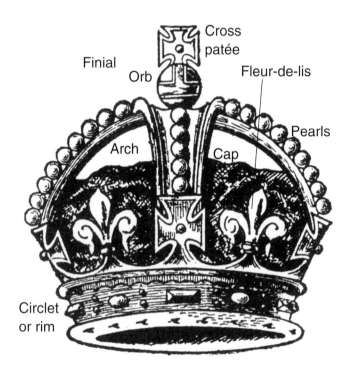

Figure 3.2 The parts of a crown. This the Royal, or St. Edward's, crown of England was made for the coronation of Charles II in 1662 by Sir Robert Vyner. It has two complete arches which cross one another—arches may also only go halfway across (figure 3.6).

The ring of white fur, usually ermine, below the circlet is the miniver. It is usually attached to a velvet cap which is separate from but ensuite with the crown. Caps may also be permanently fixed to the insides of crowns and coronets.

Arthur Charles Fox-Davies, *A Complete Guide to Heraldry* (London: T. C. & E. C. Jack, 1909), page 359, fig. 642.

dominance of the crown is in part because stylized imitations can readily be turned. Over the centuries the variety of real crowns (figures 3.2 to 3.8) has increased, as has the number of their parts. One part which is often wrongly named is the surmounting cross (figure 3.9).

THE CROWN
The crown is descended from the diadem, an ornamented and decorated bandeau worn as a badge of office. The "bandeau or fillet tied round the head was probably first used to keep long hair from getting into the eyes of primitive man".[3] Being worn high on the head and therefore visible in battle, the bandeau and the related wreath (a headpiece in the form of a bandeau made by interweaving small branches) became means to display status.

Crowns were and are worn alone, they were also worn on the helmets of armor. They are made of precious materials to reinforce their association with wealth and power. Thus crowns made of worthless or humble materials, for example Jesus' crown of thorns, were intended to ridicule their recipients.

A crown is worn by a sovereign or ruler. In some kingdoms crowns are also worn by the consort. A coronet is physically a crown, but is a badge of "lower" status than that of sovereign or consort. To call a consort queen's crown a coronet as some descriptions of the Staunton design do is therefore wrong.

The formalization of the designs of coronets, who could wear what crowns and coronets, and on what occasions, started in English heraldry during the reign of Charles II (1660–1685). The design and usage of crowns and coronets of course varies from monarchy to monarchy.

The use of regal symbols in chess has been affected by the overthrow of a monarchy—in France after the 1789 Revolution it was decreed that the king and queen chess pieces should be replaced by a flag and an adjutant respectively.

Figure 3.3 A pointed crown consisting of a circlet (also called a rim, or if very narrow a fillet) heightened with points (or spikes), and without a cap or arches. This open form is called an Eastern crown in English heraldry, and is also called the antique, heathen or David's crown. There were usually twelve points recalling the twelve rays (months) of the sun. When the crown is intended to be David's, perhaps the twelve points recall the twelve tribes of Israel.

Illustration from *A Complete Guide to Heraldry*, page 377, fig. 659.

Figure 3.5 A crown with arches, that of Henry VII of England (reigned 1485–1509) shown on a contemporary coin. The arches almost lie on a cone. Fleurs-de-lis separated by points rise from the circlet.

Illustration from *A Complete Guide to Heraldry*, page 355, fig. 634.

Figure 3.4 A crown with high points tipped with pearls, and with an internal cap, that of the Dukes of Sweden.

Illustration from Arthur Charles Fox-Davies, *The Art of Heraldry* (1904; reprint, New York, Arno Press, 1976), page 273, fig. 748.

Figure 3.6 Definitely crown-like in form, but a coronet, that of the Prince of Wales. It belongs to the prince as the eldest son of the sovereign, not as Prince of Wales. In English heraldry the term crown therefore defines the role rather than the detailed form. This coronet has two arches which join under the orb, not one complete arch.

Illustration from *The Art of Heraldry*, page 274, fig. 756.

Figure 3.7   A crown resembling a cap, the Crown of Taurien (the Crimea). This form of crown seems to have been commonly imitated in chess sets from central and eastern Europe. This crown is topped by a cross formée with pearls.

Illustration from *The Art of Heraldry*, page 272, fig. 740.

Figure 3.8   An unusually tall crown, that of Siam.
Illustration from *The Art of Heraldry*, page 273, fig. 752.

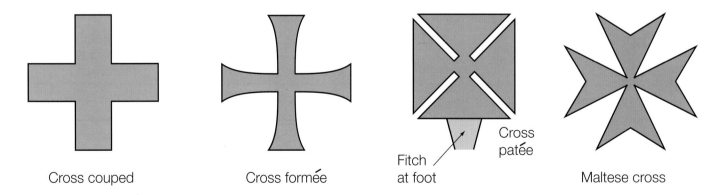

Cross couped   Cross formée   Fitch at foot   Cross patée   Maltese cross

Figure 3.9   Four of the many named variants of heraldic cross.
The cross patée (paty or patonce) is often confused with the Maltese or eight-pointed cross. The Maltese cross was the badge of the Knights of Saint John of Jerusalem, also known as the Hospitallers. In 1530 Malta was ceded to them. They ruled it, except for the period 1798 to 1802 when it was held by France, until it became a British possession by the Treaty of Paris of 1814.

3.2 QUEEN PIECE SYMBOLS

The queen's piece symbol is customarily a sphere or a crown (figure 3.10).

Early spheres may have imitated that lesser-known item of regalia, the orb, but many later spheres were instead copies of earlier spheres, the association with the orb having been forgotten. Thus the relatively-large sphere became a customary, purely-geometric, queen piece symbol (figure 3.10B). Small spheres are often found atop the crowns of both chess kings and queens (figure 3.10, D and E).

The crowns of queens and empresses are not obviously feminine when compared with kings' crowns (figure 3.11), so the chess queen's crown has usually been smaller than and different in form to the chess king's crown (figure 3.10, D and E).

Man Ray's exploitation of the medieval pointed hat worn by medieval ladies was a notable if obscure departure from the customary (figure 1.63).

Figure 3.11 The crown of the Empress of Russia. It is similar to the Emperor of Russia's crown, and to the Crown of Poland.

Illustration from *The Art of Heraldry*, page 271, fig. 735.

| B | C | D | E | F | | G | H |

Figure 3.10 Queens and a Staunton king.

B, a sphere-topped St. George queen (the set is shown in figures 4.24 and 5.7).

C, a French eighteenth-century queen with a crown with points. As figure 5.9 shows, the king also has a pointed crown, but with an orb.

D, a Staunton queen with a crown with twelve points without pearls, without arches, and an orb.

E, a Staunton king with a stylized imitation of an arched crown topped by a suggestion of an orb and a cross patée. Since the introduction of the Staunton design in 1849, the representation of a king by an arched crown and a queen by a pointed crown has become customary (figure 1.59 shows the six Staunton pieces).

F, a Philidor queen with a modest pointed crown (the six Philidor pieces are shown in figure 1.47).

G, a Stamma queen with a crown with a sharp but unbroken rim to suggest a pointed crown (the six Stamma pieces are shown in figure 2.15).

H, a Cessolis queen. Again the unbroken sharp rim represents a pointed crown (the six Cessolis pieces are shown in figure 2.14).

3.3 BISHOP PIECE SYMBOLS

The miter is a common, Western, bishop piece symbol. I don't know whether the low Gothic miters worn by the twelfth-century, Norwegian-made, Lewis bishops are derived from the gable roofs over church naves (figure 1.10), whether this form of miter was worn in other parts of Europe at the same time, or when, where and how the much taller Roman miter was introduced (figure 3.12). However the miter is only one of several forms of hat of office and other vestments worn by senior churchmen which were and could be imitated

to create bishop piece symbols (figures 3.13 and 3.14).

The miter piece symbol is usually produced by cutting a channel of rectangular, or V-shaped cross section, either sloping, vertical, or helical into a turned form resembling an upright turnip (figure 3.14). The bottom of the channel in longitudinal section may be flat or an inverted vee. The spreading bifurcated piece symbol of the Caxton bishops (figure 1.16) could have been a miter, or the hat of a fool or jester, *fou* being the French name for piece known as a bishop by English-speakers. The English translation of the German piece name for a bishop is a 'runner'. We should be cautious therefore in ascribing clerical associations to the piece

Figure 3.12 "The Bishop" wearing a miter and holding a crosier.
Illustration from Jost Amman and Hans Sachs, *Ständebuch (The Book of Trades)*, (Nuremberg, 1568; reprint, New York: Dover Publications, 1973), page 11.

Figure 3.13 "The Cardinal" wearing a hat which is not a miter. Different hats were worn by senior churchmen in different regions at different times, and for different occasions.
Illustration from *The Book of Trades*, page 10.

symbols of bishops in sets from mainland Europe.

The French piece symbols used for bishops in eighteenth- and nineteenth-century turned sets do not obviously seem to imitate any part of a jester's dress or equipment. This has contributed to a widespread confusion among English-speaking users and collectors of these sets which has resulted in French bishops being wrongly identified as knights and vice versa. An important article by Franz Josef Lang clarifies the differences between bishops and knights in such sets:[4]

1. The knight is taller than the bishop (figures 3.15, also figures 1.31 and 5.9).
2. The bishop's head may be facetted (fig 1.31, but contrast the facetted knight in figure 3.28), or be a knob-like finial within a high rim which is partially cut away (figure 3.15).
3. The knight's head may be a small, tall dome (figures 1.31 and 3.15), although central-European bishops may also use tall dome piece symbols.[6]

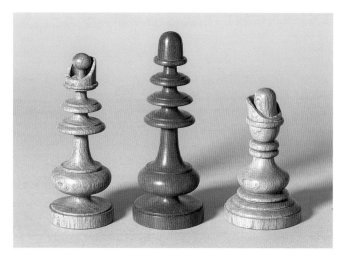

Figure 3.15   The confusion of turned French bishops and knights. *Left*, a copy of an eighteenth-century French bishop; *center*, a copy of a knight from the same set;[5] *right*, a copy of a German or Austrian early-nineteenth-century bishop which is clearly a bishop because there are also horse-headed knights in the set. The sets are pictured in figures 5.9, and 1.39 and 5.6, respectively.

Figure 3.14   Bishop's hat piece symbols.

B, a copy of an Eastern-European bishop, the original is in Gareth Williams, *Master Pieces*, page 76.

C, a copy of an Austrian bishop, the original is pictured in Gareth Williams, *Master Pieces*, page 130.

D, a Staunton bishop. Its miter has a pearl, and an offset and canted channel of rectangular cross section. I don't know whether the cant of the channel is supposed to echo the piece's diagonal movement. The six pieces of the set are shown in figure 1.59.

E, a St. George bishop with a small bun turned at the top of the miter so that the tops of the miter are not sharp (the six St. George pieces are shown in figures 4.24 and 5.7).

F, a Philidor bishop with sharp tops to its miter (the six Philidor pieces are shown in figure 1.47).

3.4   KNIGHT PIECE SYMBOLS

The chaturangan knight imitated a cavalryman on his horse. This symbolism continues to today, and in most recent, Western sets the knight is the only piece which retains an figurative piece symbol. This is usually a horse's head and neck, but may include more or all of a horse's body and legs. The facial expressions of knight horses have included fierce, terrified, happy, puzzled, and shy, but the first two are the most appropriate for horses involved in war.

Only a horse symbol which has been well-carved, both technically and aesthetically, complements a well-turned set. To ensure a fine head, the early Staunton horse heads were based on those in the Elgin marbles (figure 3.16). Later Jaques' Staunton horse heads were less vigorous (figure 3.17).

Figures 3.18 and 3.19 are intended to assist those who wish to carve horse heads. If you are not confident that you can carve horse heads to the appropriate standard, you could consider

1. A stylized equine piece signature which is easier to produce than an accurate imitation, and can be just as effective (figures 3.20 and 3.21).
2. An accurate or stylized imitation of another part of a horse, such as a hoof or horseshoe,
3. An accurate or stylized imitation of a knightly or cavalry accoutrement other than a horse. Possibilities include helms, helmets, shields, lances, stirrups or other parts of saddles (figures 3.22 to 3.27).
4. Military accoutrements and objects both earlier and later than medieval.
5. A piece signature which represents the knight's "diagonal" movement (figures 3.28B and D). Other

Figure 3.16   Horses sculpted in low relief on a part of the frieze of the Parthenon, Athens, now in the British Museum. These had been removed from the Acropolis in 1801-3 by 7th Earl of Elgin, and in 1816 sold by him to the British Museum for 35,000 pounds.

The booklet *John Jaques 1795–1995* quotes from the *Morning Herald* of 6th November, 1849: "The crude, ugly and ill-cut caricature now in use is supplanted by an exquisite draft of the head of the Greek horse executed after the Elgin marbles . . . They may be viewed and judged as works of art, and as such challenge scrutiny; while the beauty of the manufacture is indicative of the high perfection to which ivory carving and the niceties of ivory turning have been brought in this country."

Illustration from *Description of the Collection of Ancient Marbles in the British Museum; with Engravings*, part VIII (London: Trustees of the British Museum, 1839), plate XVII opposite page 119.

examples include the knights designed by Frederick Copley (figure 1.57), Man Ray (figure 1.63), and Yves Tanguy (figure 1.64). The knight is also the only piece which moves *over* other chessmen, a property which does not seem to have been exploited for piece symbols—although the forms of the early Russian knight in figure 1.14 and Man Ray's knight perhaps suggest the ability to leap over.

Figure 3.18   Views of a horse's head and neck.
The horse, Khatir Asbaa (Baby), had to be bribed with carrots to pose by her owner Mrs. Debra Burton.

Figure 3.17   A twentieth-century, boxwood, Jaques, Staunton knight.

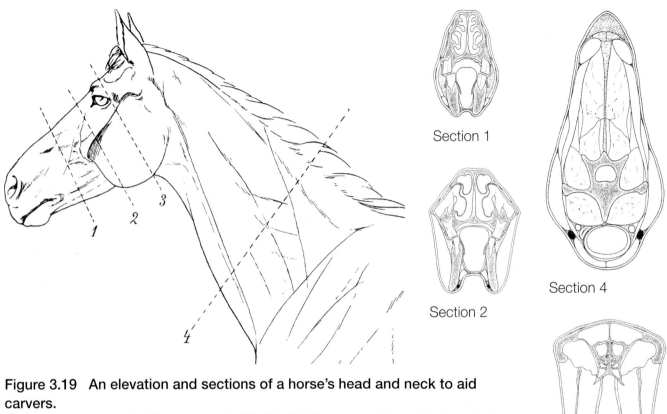

Section 1

Section 2

Section 4

Section 3

Figure 3.19   An elevation and sections of a horse's head and neck to aid carvers.

Illustrations from W. Ellenberger, H. Dittrich, H. Baum, *An Atlas of Animal Anatomy for Artists* (New York: Dover Publications), 1956.

Figure 3.20   Stylized verses poorly imitated horse heads. *Center*, a horse's head resembling a kangaroo's from the barleycorn set in figure 1.36; *left and right*, much more effective Russian stylized horse heads also shown on pages 123 and 124.

Figure 3.21   Stylized (or just crudely carved?) horse heads from the French set shown in figure 1.32.

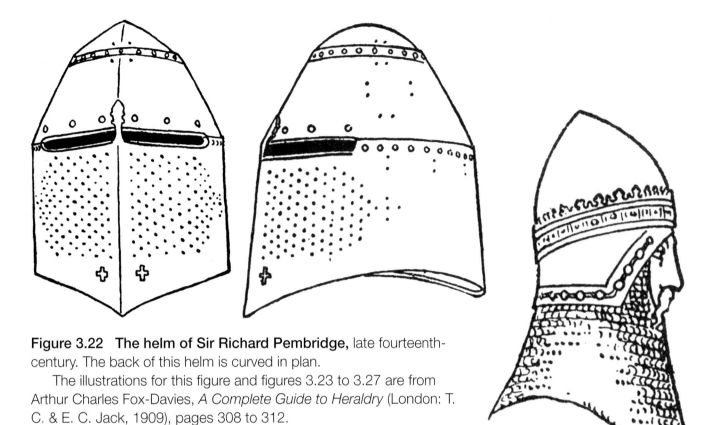

Figure 3.22   The helm of Sir Richard Pembridge, late fourteenth-century. The back of this helm is curved in plan.

   The illustrations for this figure and figures 3.23 to 3.27 are from Arthur Charles Fox-Davies, *A Complete Guide to Heraldry* (London: T. C. & E. C. Jack, 1909), pages 308 to 312.

Figure 3.24   The basinet, introduced in France late in the thirteenth century.

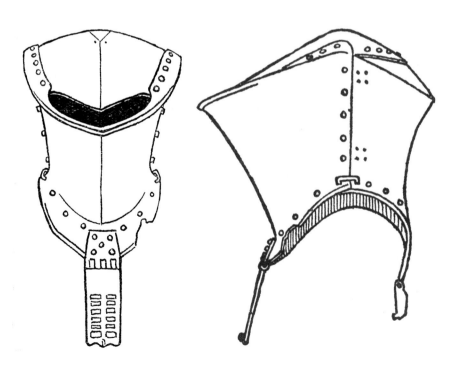

Figure 3.23   A jousting-helm, front and side elevations .

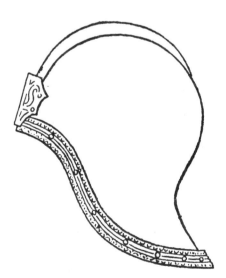

Figure 3.25   A celata.

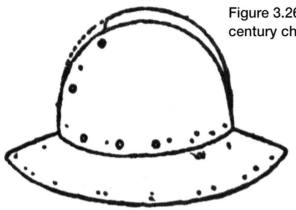

Figure 3.26 A late-fifteenth-century chapelle-de-fer.

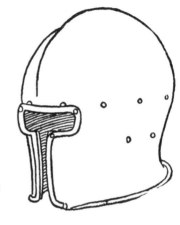

Figure 3.27   An Italian celata.

B   C   D   E   F   G

Figure 3.28 Knights with different piece symbols.

B, a knight cut aslant (the set's six pieces are shown in figures 1.35 and 5.4). H. J. R. Murray quotes two sources for this symbol: "the knight hath his top cut asloope, as thoughe beynge dubbed knight",[7] and "like a feather in a helmet".[8] If the first source is valid, the sovereign must have been an unusually vigorous and inaccurate dubber. Nor is the feather explanation convincing. Could the sloping cut represent the knight's "diagonal" movement?

C, a copy of a French, eighteenth-century knight (the set's six pieces are shown in figure 5.9).

D, a copy of the facetted knight from an English, late-seventeenth-century set pictured in Gareth Williams, *Master Pieces*, pages 48 and 49. Williams states, "The knight has a triangular finial, probably to indicate a tricorn [hat] as worn by a gentleman squire". The facetted top could also represent the knight's diagonal movement, or be copied from the contemporary, French, facetted bishop which was frequently thought to be a knight by the British (figure 1.31).

E, a typical horse-headed knight (the set's six pieces are shown in figure 1.50).

F, a Stamma knight topped by a pot-helmet (the set's six pieces are shown in figure 2.15).

G, a knight wearing a shako cavalry helmet.

3.5 ROOK PIECE SYMBOLS

Rooks were originally carved imitations of horsedrawn war chariots. The Spanish Alfonso MS of 1283 instructs that the carved rook should imitate a mass of horsemen crowded together.[9] The earliest recorded appearance of the current Western piece symbol, the castle tower, was in 1524, and is reproduced in figure 1.21.

Although in contemporary English *rook* is preferred to *castle*, the latter piece name is recalled in the special moves of *castling*. In this sixteenth-century innovation the king moves three squares to its right or left, and the castle to the king's right or left moves to the square on the far side of the repositioned king. The word castle is derived from the castellum, a derivative of the Latin *castrum*, 'a fortified place' which was both a private residence and fortress. In French and German the rook's piece name is castle tower (*tour* and *turm* respectively). In Russian carved sets the rook is carved to imitate a "lada" (boat). This may have arisen because many smaller Russian boats could be wheeled when necessary. However most of the carved lada chessmen resemble ocean-going sailing ships which were far too large to be amphibious.

CASTLE TOWERS

Stone castles started to be built in Europe in the eleventh century. During the Crusades (A.D. 1095–1291), the European adventurers saw the hugely-impressive fortresses and city walls (ramparts) built by the Byzantines, notably the Theodosian land walls at Constantinople built between A.D. 404 and 413. As a result the Norman motte-and-bailey castle design was developed and strengthened using double and triple concentric curtain walls with bastions (towers incorporated into the walls). Although weapons which used gunpowder were introduced in the mid-fourteenth century, they were ineffective against castles until Henry V's cannon battered down the walls of Harfleur in 1415. The development of siege guns continued, and among those the Turks used to batter down the walls of Constantinople in 1453 was one weighing 19 tons (19.3 tonnes) which could fire a stone ball of 1500 pounds (680 kg) a mile (1.6 km). Thereafter castles became increasingly obsolete.

A castle tower which stands alone is a keep, or in Norman-French a donjon. Although usually square or rectangular in plan; they could also be round in plan. A bartizan is a small overhanging turret which projects from the angles on the top of a tower, or from the parapet or other parts of a building (figure 3.29).

Most castle towers had vertical or slightly battered walls. Their stonework was fairly smooth to prevent besiegers climbing up it. However in rooks, prominent V-cuts are often used to imitate horizontal joints, and less-often vertical joints, between the ashlars.

Tops of towers sometimes projected horizontally to to permit machicolations (figure 3.30). Such projections also made it more difficult for besiegers to push the tops of siege ladders high enough to access the alurs. Tower tops were also usually embattled (figure 3.31 to 3.33).

DESIGNING ROOKS

When a rook incorporates a castle tower, the whole of the rook's form may be tower. Alternatively the tower may be supported, often on a part-group incorporating a baluster. Chess castle towers may carry an object such as a flag or a gun. Many forms of castle tower, both real and imaginary, have been used in rooks (figure 3.34). Other metaphors for security and strength have also been adopted for rooks; for example, skyscrapers, and bridge pylons.

There is usually an even number (four, six, or eight) of crenels or embrasures in a rook battlement. Four is the most logical number because it echoes the four directions at right angles in which a rook can move.

Figure 3.29 A bartizan (turret or tourelle), here crenellated. A building with a row of turrets is turriculated.

Illustration from J. Henry Parker, *Classic Dictionary of Architecture* (1875; reprint, Poole, Dorset; New Orchard Editions, 1986), pages 29–30.

Figure 3.31   A battlement is an indented parapet. The upward projections of a battlement are merlons. If the gaps between the merlons are narrow as here, the gaps are embrasures. When the gaps are similar in width to the merlons or wider they are called crenels (or crenelles).

A building with battlements is said to be crenellated or castellated. A royal licence (a kernellare) was required in medieval times before a subject could build a castle or fortify an existing structure.

Illustration from J. Henry Parker, *Classic Dictionary of Architecture*, page 36.

Figure 3.30   The parts of a castle tower's or wall's upper projection.

A, an alur, a passage, gallery, walkway or similar running behind a parapet. The alur may be roofed, as here, or be without a roof. Chess rooks commonly have a circular alur surrounded by a battlement.

B, a battlement.

C, corbels, brackets which support the battlement, and often the floor of the alur.

M, a machicolation, an opening in the floor of the alur through which boiling oil, stones, and other injurious things could be poured, dropped, or fired onto attackers without the defenders being exposed.

Illustration from J. Henry Parker, *Classic Dictionary of Architecture*, page 9.

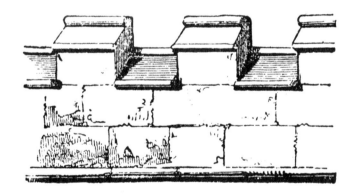

Figure 3.32   The top surfaces of the merlons and the surfaces forming the bottoms of the embrasures or cresnels were often sloped to shed water. The sloping bottom surfaces of the cresnels also enabled defenders to more easily fire arrows, drop objects, or pour liquids onto those below, and made it more difficult for attackers to access the alur from siege ladders.

Illustration from Cyril M.Harris, *Illustrated Dictionary of Historic Architecture* (New York: Dover Publications, 1983), page 55.

Figure 3.33 V-shaped embrasures in merlons at Verona, Italy. Merlons of this form are carved on the rooks of an eighteenth-century, central-European set pictured on page 102 of Alex Hammond, *The Book of Chessmen*. Could the resemblance of these merlons to the tops of the rooks introduced into Europe by the Moors (figure 1.4) have influenced the introduction of the castle tower as the symbol for rook?

Illustration from Cyril M. Harris, *Illustrated Dictionary of Historic Architecture*, New York: Dover Publications, 1983, page 55.

Figure 3.34 Six rooks.

B, a French eighteenth-century rook (the set's six pieces are shown in figure 5.9). The simple tapering castle tower with a projecting battlement is the most common rook piece symbol.

C, domed and two-story, based loosely on an ivory rook pictured in Gareth Williams, *Master Pieces*, page 103.

D, a copy of a nineteenth-century, Italian, ivory rook shown in Frank Greygoose, *Chessmen*, page 91.

E, a copy of a Rockingham ceramic rook pictured in chapter VIII of Donald M. Liddell, *Chessmen*.

F, a copy of Marcel Duchamp's directional rook of 1919 (see also figure 1.62).

G, a Stamma rook. Its conical roof and that of rook E are called a spire. The set's six pieces are shown in figure 2.15.

3.6 PAWN PIECE SYMBOLS

Chaturangan pawns were carved to imitate infantrymen. The term *pawn* recalls that role, although the word's meaning outside chess is "minor or subservient person". In figuratively carved chessmen, pawns have often been carved as workers or other members of the lower strata of society. The modesty of the roles represented by pawns and the pawn's lack of power in chess is reflected by pawns usually being the shortest and least ornamented and decorated men in a set. The only common turned piece symbol for a pawn is the sphere (which is not an orb), but many turned pawns are without them (figure 3.35).

Figure 3.35 Pawns based on two central-European, early-nineteenth-century pawns pictured in Gareth Williams, *Master Pieces*, pages 74 and 75. The wood is yellow carabeen.

3.7 ENDNOTES

1. Gareth Williams, *The Amazing Book of Chess* (London: Tiger Books, 1995), p. 20.

2. Mike Darlow, *Woodturning Design*, pp. 5-7, 54. The sense was earlier introduced in E. H. Gombrich, *The Sense of Order* (London: Phaidon Press, 1979).

3. Arthur Charles Fox-Davies, *A Complete Guide to Heraldry* (London: T. C. & E. C. Jack, 1909), p. 350.

4. Franz Josef Lang "French Playing Sets of the 18th and 19th Centuries," *The Chess Collector* (March 1989): pp. 3–6, 11. To prove his point Lang reproduces eighteenth- and nineteenth-century French and English engravings.

5. The originals on which the copies are based are pictured on page 18 of Mackett-Beeson, *Chessmen*, and on page 48 of F. Lanier Graham, *Chess Sets*. In both books the bishops are wrongly identified as knights, and vice versa.

6. Gareth Williams, *Master Pieces*, pp. 64 and 65.

7. H. J. R. Murray, *A History of Chess*, p. 772, quoted from the 1562 Rowbothum translation of Damiano.

8. H. J. R. Murray, p. 773, quoted from Rundle Holme, *Academy of Armory* (1681–82).

9. H. J. R. Murray, p. 769.

Chapter Four

DESIGNING CHESS SETS

Only one chess-set design, now over 150 years old, is approved for use in world championships:

> The preferred chess set has the following specifications: A board with squares 5 cm x 5 cm ... The pawn should have a base with a width equal to one half the size of the square [i.e. the pawn base diameter should be 2.5 cm] ... The height of the rook should be equal to the diagonal of the square [i.e. rooks should be 5 x 1.414 = 7 cm tall] ... The shape of the pieces should correspond to the Staunton design ... In tournaments where players supply their own equipment, the arbiter decides which of the chess sets is closer in design to the preferred set described above.[1]

This restriction was introduced to remove a possible issue for conflict between players in an unusually stressful situation. Has it though allowed the sensitivities of a few to repress the introduction of fresh chess-set designs in recent decades? I don't think so. But I do believe that there should be greater encouragement for the designing of contemporary chess sets, and stronger, more overt, and more informed criticism of those designs. This chapter is especially relevant to both aims, which, if realized, will bolster the interest in chess playing.

4.1 INCEPTION

The process for designing a chess set, shown in figures 4.1 and 4.2, starts with an inception. Chancing upon this book may be such a trigger. Other examples are

1. An approach from a client.
2. A desire to enter a competition.
3. A desire to give a present.
4. Seeing a chess set which inspires you to copy it, or produce an improved version.
5. The emergence of an idea, often a fresh combination of preexistent ideas; or the realization

that a restraint can be ignored. An example of the fresh, single idea is the invention of magnetic chessmen.
6. The realization that some particular wood or other materials or components would be especially suitable to be made into chessmen.
7. A desire to trial or practice a new technique or piece of equipment.

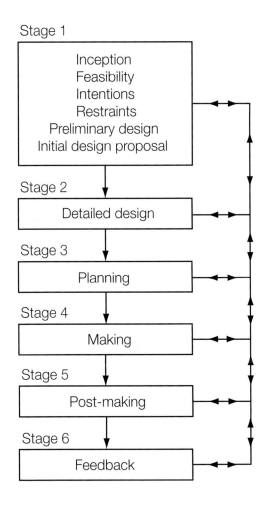

Figure 4.1 A flow chart of the stages for the creation of a man-made object. Stage 1 is expanded in the next figure. Stage 5 may include packing, transport, exhibition, and selling.

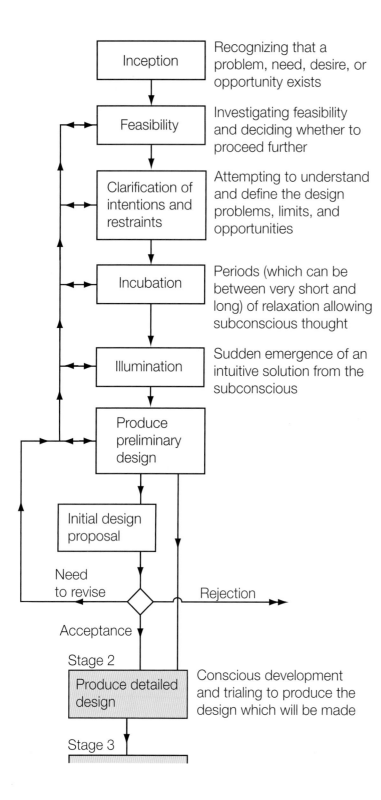

Figure 4.2 An expanded flow chart for stage 1 of the design process. Here, as in figure 4.1, the certitude that designing includes reassessing earlier information and decisions, and working through subsequent steps again is shown by the paths and arrows outside the labelled rectangles.

4.2 FEASIBILITY

After the inception you should consciously decide whether to proceed with the rest of the stage I design. Factors which may influence this decision include

1. Is the inceptive idea as clever as you first thought?
2. Is the client's budget sufficient?
3. Do you have the interest, the skills, and the other required resources, including time? Can you source the resources which you need, but don't have now?

Fortunately, chessmen are usually small, and need not require much expenditure on materials; nor does making them have to require technically complex and therefore expensive equipment. You can also decide during the design stage what level of workmanship will be needed, and consequently the time required to make the chess set. This time is usually measured in hours or days rather than weeks.

4.3 INTENTIONS

Every chessman has properties which can be sensed. These include form (which is independent of size, and includes three-dimensional ornament), size (particularly height and maximum diameter), weight, stability, color, surface texture, and surface glossiness. You should design and specify these properties so that each chessman in the set satisfies your intentions as well as possible. The book *Woodturning Design* defines and discusses seven types of intention which can apply to the design of a man-made object:

1. *Reproductive*, concerned with the need or desire to produce copies or replacements.
2. *Functional*, concerned with use ("playability").
3. *Economic*, concerned with the cost, the resources needed for production, and the sale price.

4. *Aesthetic*, primarily concerned with appearance and feel.

5. *Communicative*, primarily concerned with how well a chessman communicates which set and side it belongs to, and what piece it is.

6. *Focussed on the materials, techniques, and equipment used in the making of the set.*

7. *Personal.* Chessmen and chess sets may be designed and produced for reasons which were not intended to become known to the public at the time. For example, if chessmen were made in the course of practicing a new technique and then thrown away, someone who found them would be wrong to conclude that the workmanship displayed represented the best that their maker could achieve.

I discuss these seven types of intention in more detail below.

4.3.1 REPRODUCTIVE INTENTIONS

The intention to copy chessmen or parts of chessmen is reproductive. The intention to work in a particular defined style is also reproductive, and may result from an aesthetic and/or a communicative intention.

4.3.2 FUNCTIONAL INTENTIONS

The playability and convenience of chess sets depend on:

1. *Stability*. Although the height:base-diameter ratio is a rough measure of a chessman's stability, the way the weight is distributed within a man is also material (figures 4.3 and 4.4). In figure 4.4, however, the stability associated with a relatively large base diameter is sacrificed to enable self-righting.

   Stability is not the only factor which should determine whether you should lead a set, and if so, how much lead should be put into each man—the aesthetic pleasure of moving chessmen during a game depends on their weights.

   Related to stability is the need for the men of travelling sets to remain in position on the board during the exigencies of travel (figures 4.5 and 4.6). Similarly, the magnets of magnetic chessmen should be strong enough for the men to remain in place in normal circumstances, but not be so strong that the chessmen cannot be readily moved.

2. *Set, side and piece identification.* A chessman cannot fulfill the functional intention of playability unless it communicates which side it belongs to, what piece it is, and what set it belongs to so that it does not become mixed into a different set. The functional intention of playability cannot therefore be satisfied unless the related communicative intentions are, and these are discussed later in subsection 4.3.5.

Figure 4.3 Two chessmen with the same ratio of height:maximum diameter, but different stabilities. The stability of the left-hand men could be further improved by leading; the base of the bone man on the right is too thin to permit leading.

If a chessman is made from one material, the height of its center of gravity is not affected by the density of that material. However more force is needed to knock over a heavy chessmen than a lighter one of the same form.

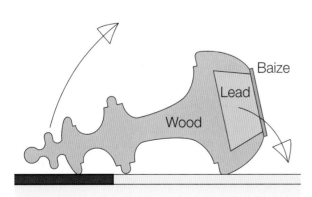

Figure 4.4 Self-righting, Schmitthenner chessmen which stand back up if knocked over because of their heavy leading and base shape. *Bottom left,* this drawing explains the self-righting feature, and is based on a diagram in 1887 U.S. Patent 361,721 issued to L. S. Schmitthenner, reproduced in "Travel Chess at the Russian Chess Museum" by Natalia Ivanova (*The Chess Collector*, April 1997), pages 14–15. In the article Natalia mentions that "Travel chess sets created in Russia in the second half of the nineteenth century . . . are fabricated with such heavy weights in their bases that they generally don't fall over, but only rock and sway". Then editor of *The Chess Collector*, Mike Pennell, added details of the Schmitthenner patent, and noted that there were corresponding British and German patents.

The Polumbaum Collection. Photographs by Risa Korris.

3. *Accessibility*. Having different pieces different heights aids identification, but extreme height differences make accessing and moving the shorter men more difficult. The ratio of the height of the tallest man in a set to the shortest is 1:1 for most travelling sets, and below 2:1 for most playing sets. Accessibility is also affected by the diameters of the pieces relative to the board's square size. Men which are relatively small in diameter compared to the board's square size are more accessible than men which are larger in diameter.

4. *Ease of moving*. Chessmen with definite heads and necks are easier to slide, pick up, and put down than chessmen without these features.

5. *The ability of the men of a set to occupy little volume*. This ability may be functional (figure 4.7); it may also express a designer's communicative intention to display his or her ingenuity—Josef Hartwig's Bauhaus set shown in figure 1.66 is probably an example of this.

6. *Size*. The sizes of the men in a set should be appropriate to their intended usage, which should in turn determine the size and form of the board. The men of travelling sets are small (figures 4.5 and 4.6); those used for exhibition, teaching, or public entertainment are often large (figures 4.7 to 4.9). If a set is intended to be used by seated players, reach determines the maximum size of the board and hence the sizes of the chessmen. If the designer intends players to walk around or even on the board, or if players are provided with devices akin to fishing rods to move the men, the board can be much larger than usual.

7. *Durability*. Chessmen with sharp edges, delicate protrusions, and narrow cross sections are easily damaged (figures 4.10 and 4.11). The shallow disk-like bases common on ivory or bone chessmen (figures 1.37 and 1.43) are particularly fragile if replicated in wood because of the short grain (figure 1.36). A durable design is desirable if the set is intended for frequent use, and if its men are stored in a box without individual compartments (figure 1.44).

Figure 4.5 Cattle-bone travelling chessmen by Brian Lemin of Cooranbong, New South Wales. The bone part of the king is 1$\frac{3}{8}$ in. (35 mm) tall. The cushion was made by Mrs. Jean Lemin.

Figure 4.6   A travelling chess set made in India in the 1990s. The men are plastic. The exposed heights of all the men are the same, and are just a little less than the distance from the top surface of the board to the underside of the lid when the lid is closed.

The fit between the turned lid and the base is unlikely to remain nice through time when they are cut from radially grained disks of solid wood as here.

Figure 4.7   Chessmen which are large, stable, light in weight, and nest. These "Exhibition Chessmen" were designed and patented by a Mr. Peter Toepfer. They were used by Dr. Emanuel Lasker, world chess champion from 1894 to 1921, to teach chess. The poster from which this illustration is taken explains: "The giant Chessmen are made of Aluminum and are so light that they can be readily moved when set up on the stage for games, problems, etc. After the performance they are packed within the compass of a trunk, two by four feet in size, for transportation [*back right*]. The board measures twenty feet square and is made of cloth, with black and white squares, each 30 by 30 inches. As he makes the necessary explanations, the lecturer walks out upon the board and moves the pieces as required. The Kings and Queens are all three feet six inches high."

A much smaller chess set of nesting metal cones, but with the pieces signified by the ways the tops of the cones are cut away is pictured in F. Lanier Graham, *Chess Sets*, figure 77.

Illustration from Fred Wilson, *A Picture History of Chess*, page 70, courtesy of Dover Publications.

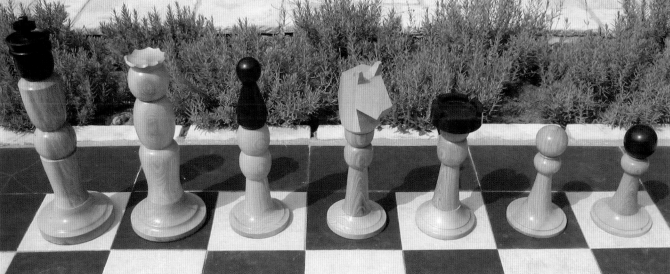

Figure 4.8   An outdoor chess set designed and turned by Jamie Wallwin for use at the Craft Supplies teaching facility in the Pyrenees area of France. The two sides are identical in form. The tops of the black side are stained black, the tops of the white side are unstained. The board is tiled.

Figure 4.9 Playing chess in Hyde Park, central Sydney. The chessmen are hollow and plastic, and therefore light, cheap, and durable.

Figure 4.10 A delicate set, eighteenth century, ivory, with large, double-headed knights, possibly turned by Anton Edel in Munich. The king is 3 1/2 in. (89 mm) high.
Polumbaum Collection. Photograph by Risa Korris.

THE **PHILIDOR** Chess-Men, designed by some of the LEAD-
ING METROPOLITAN PLAYERS with a view to FITNESS FOR ACTUAL
PLAY AND NON-LIABILITY TO BREAKAGE.—The handsome folding BOARDS, to accompany them, have squares of the colours
most suitable to the eye, and are embellished in an entirely
novel manner. *Both Men and Boards are registered.*

MEN.

	£	s.	d.		£	s.	d.
IVORY (*Club size*) ...	9	2	0	WOOD (*Club size, loaded*)	1	15	0
Do. (*Second size*) ...	4	11	0	Do. (*Second size, ditto*)	1	6	0

BOARDS.

	£	s.	d.
LARGE size	1	8	0
SECOND size	0	14	0

SETS.

	£	s.	d.
IVORY MEN, *Club size*, with Large Board	10	10	0
" *Second size*, with Second-sized Board	5	5	0
WOOD MEN, *Club size, loaded*, with Large Board	3	3	0
" *Second size, loaded*, with Second-sized Board .	2	0	0

N.B.—To the interior of the lid of every box containing these
Chess-Men is affixed a label, bearing the signature of the sole authorised
Manufacturer, G. MERRIFIELD, 33, *East Street, Queen's Square,
London*; by whom they are sold Wholesale and Retail, and from
whom Advertising Show-Cards may be had.

** Obtainable through any Chess-Men Dealer in the Kingdom, and
at the Office of the "Chess-Player's Chronicle," 21, *King William
Street, Charing Cross.*

**Figure 4.11   A set designed for "non-liability to
breakage",** so claims this advertisement for the
Philidor men (also shown in figure 1.47) in the
December, 1850, *Chessplayers Chronicle*. The
absence of thin cross sections and delicate
projections ensured durability; the leaded and
generous bases ensured stability.

Illustration kindly supplied by Gareth Williams.

4.3.3   ECONOMIC INTENTIONS

The relevant economic intention for many designers
is to achieve an acceptable input of resources rather
than a commercially acceptable sale price. The
importance of a relatively low, but still profitable, sale
price for playing sets intended to sell in large numbers
is obvious. Displaying sets may be less sensitive to
price. Some are deliberately designed to have a high
perceived value through displaying much expert
workmanship, being made of expensive materials, and/
or having an association with a well-known person or
event.

4.3.4   AESTHETIC INTENTIONS

There are many valid aesthetic intentions. You might
intend that someone who experiences your design of
chess set should feel that it is ugly, grand, delicate, or
delightful. (Delight is a lively form of beauty which
combines harmony with variety). The most common
aesthetic intention is however "this chess set shall be
beautiful".

BEAUTY
The noun *beauty* now means both 'aesthetic
commendability' and 'classical elegance'. On page 41
of *Woodturning Design* I give a description of beauty which
applies to both meanings:

> Beauty is not consequential, an inevitable
> result of solving design problems well or of
> designing purely functionally; nor is beauty an
> unpursuable by-product, something which
> occurs or does not occur according to factors
> which you cannot influence. Beauty is an
> indefinable and insufficient aim. There are
> degrees of beauty; even ugly turnings can have
> beautiful details. Many factors, not just the
> narrow concept of beauty, can combine to make
> a man-made object successful to both its
> designer and to others who may experience it.

Not everyone agrees that a particular object is
equally beautiful, nor does its perceived beauty remain
constant through time (figure 4.12). The eighteenth-

century philosophers David Hume and Immanuel Kant stated that there are standards of taste, that there is broad agreement on what is beautiful and what is not. These standards vary through time and with place, and are influenced by fashion. If there were no standards of taste, books offering guidance on designing for beauty would be pointless.

Hume's and Kant's view that there are standards of taste does not deny the validity of differences between individual tastes as long as those differences lie within the ranges of the standards. Thus judgements on beauty cannot be wholly subjective. The "Well, I like it" excuse trotted out by those who have produced something ugly when they intended to produce something beautiful should not therefore be blindly accepted.

BEAUTY OF FORM

The meanings of *form* and of other terms useful for design discussions are clarified in figures 4.13 to 4.15. Form is usually the most important factor determining how we react aesthetically to chess sets and chessmen, and the most important contributor to the beauty of form is often said to be proportion.

PROPORTION

There is a popular view that beauty is guaranteed if an object's overall proportion of height to maximum width or diameter conforms to one of the "favored" ratios such as those of the Golden proportion (1.618:1) or the Fibonacci series. The merit of these favored ratios is supposedly validated by their mathematical nicety, and because the proportions of some beautiful natural objects conform. I show on pages 47 to 51 of *Woodturning Design* that the only truth in this view is that these lauded proportions are mathematically nice. I further show that the overall proportion of an object has little to do with its beauty, but does influence other aesthetic properties such as "strikingness", a perception that an object's proportions are unusual. For example, sports cars are customarily long and low, but whether the ratio of a sports car's length:height is

Figure 4.12 Variation in taste. This eighteenth-century, Austrian design might not be to everyone's taste today despite its superb workmanship. However this rare design with its double-headed knights was probably fashionable and therefore much admired when it was made. The king is 3⅝ in. (92 mm) high.
Polumbaum Collection. Photograph Risa Korris.

4.0:1.0, 4.1:1.0, or 4.2:1.0 will not perceptibly affect its beauty. Can a sports car with the proportion 1.5:1.0 be beautiful? Yes, because there are beautiful motor vehicles with this proportion, but the ratio is not customary for sports cars because of the functional need for low air resistance and good roadholding. However, imposing an overall proportion which is far from customary will require changes to the object's customary number and/or proportions of parts (figure 4.16).

Overall proportions can affect our aesthetic reactions in particular circumstances. A sphere has the proportion 1.0:1.0:1.0. An object topped by a similar form with the proportion 1.0:1.05:1.05 would be perceived as being topped by an imperfect sphere rather than being topped by a form unrelated to the sphere. Further, the imperfect-sphere perception would adversely affect the viewer's perception of the beauty of the object even though the object would not be intrinsically less beautiful.

What about an object's internal proportions? To measure internal proportions an object has to be divided into parts. Sizing these parts according to any of the favored proportions does not guarantee beauty. This does not mean that you should not use the favored proportions, merely that there are an infinite number of other proportions which will yield similar beauty.

If imposing particular, favored, external and internal proportions does not guarantee beauty, what does? The search for beauty or the satisfaction of any aesthetic intention is essentially a process of trial and error which does not have one, best, exact solution. William Hogarth in his 1753 book *The Analysis of Beauty* called designing for beauty by trial and error the "art of composing well".

The most important recent text on "composing well" is Roger Scruton's *The Aesthetics of Architecture* (Princeton, NJ: Princeton University Press, 1979). It explains on page 235 that an object has appropriate proportions when its "parts–judged in terms of their shape and size–provide adequate visual reason for one another". But, stresses Scruton, the search for "adequate visual reason" by trial and error with the sizes and proportions of the frames or boxes encasing parts, and with the shapes of the parts within, is too narrow because it ignores the role of detail.

DETAIL
A detail is defined in the legend of figure 4.13. Roger Scruton makes the following points about details:[3]

1. Details solve practical or aesthetic problems. A designer needs to appreciate that there is a problem requiring solution before he or she can solve it.
2. The designs of details are often dictated by the means of production. Turned details have characteristic form. Some turning techniques, multi-axis turning for example, have been developed which disguise the fact that they are lathe-based.
3. Our response to a detail may be inseparable from our perception of its method of production. We may admire a surface with tool marks because it is the "memorial of an activity" which leads us to empathize with the carver.
4. A detail can be appreciated for itself, but should also make a positive contribution to the whole.
5. The absence of detail causes us to search for smaller-scale detail. Thus we notice the smallest imperfection on a flat, highly polished surface.
6. Conformance to a geometrically defined form can be important in a detail. (This was discussed in the preceding column using the example of a perfect sphere and an "imperfect sphere").

An appreciation of detail thus underpins how we judge objects aesthetically. Roger Scruton called this facility *the sense of detail*. We use it to search for and improve detail, and to make aesthetic judgements, judgements which often use information stored in memory. But the sense of detail is not the only relevant conceptual sense; the late Sir Ernst Gombrich postulated two more senses to simplify discussing how we react to objects:

1. *The sense of order* is the process of repeated questioning of just-sensed information on the basis of order, with order being defined by information already held in memory. For example, if you saw a chess set which had its piece heights graded from the shortest, the king, up to the tallest, the pawn, your sense of order would be jolted.
2. *The sense of meaning* is similar to the sense of order,

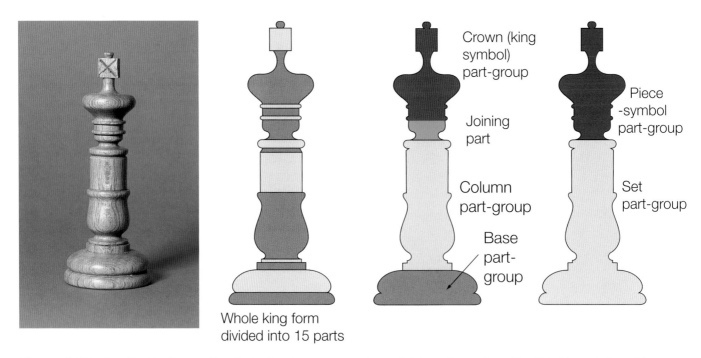

Whole king form
divided into 15 parts

Figure 4.13 **Aesthetic terms illustrated** using a copy of an eighteenth-century English king pictured in Michael Mark, *British Chess Sets*, 1996, exhibit 27.

1. *Form* means 'shape'; it is independent of size, color, material, or meaning. The outside surfaces of textures are strictly part of the form, but are generally considered separately.
2. *Ornament* is three-dimensional detail which is applied to, or subtracted from, the unornamented form, and which can be "enjoyed and appreciated independently of any dominant aesthetic whole".[2] Moldings are the most common turned ornaments.
3. *Moldings* are three-dimensional and "linear"; they run along, around, or helically along and around the unornamented form. Moldings are often used to define and emphasize structure and articulate boundaries between parts. Some common moldings are defined in figure 4.14.
4. *Decoration* is essentially two-dimensional, and results from the application of paint, stain, leaf, or polish. If you select a material because of its organic color and pattern, or if you specify a gloss level, you are decorating. In this context *organic* means 'intrinsic to the material'; it has nothing to do with life or with carbon. Rocks and metals therefore have organic color.
5. A *part* is the smallest, single entity of volume. The boundary between two adjacent parts is usually along a discontinuity in the form's surface; it may also be chosen to be along the line at which the curvature of the form's surface changes from convex to concave (a plane of inflection), or where the curvature is particularly tight (figure 4.15).
6. A *part-group* is one part, or a group of connected parts, which together possess a distinct form. A part-group is also often a nameable entity within a chessman's overall form.
7. A *detail* is an area which you focus on, which you conceptually isolate and study. It can also be an area which you are likely to focus on. You may be attracted to investigate a detail, or may focus on a detail while progressing through a deliberate design procedure. Although a small part, a part of a part, a combination of the two, a molding, an ornament, an area of decoration, the exact shape of a curve, or the meeting of two parts can be a detail, a feature or an area does not become a detail until you focus on it. There can be a hierarchy of detail; a detail may be composed of smaller details, which in turn may be composed of still smaller details.
8. The *style* is essentially the organizing principal for the design. It can be a recognizable and named style.

but is concerned with what the just-sensed input means, again by comparing it to information relating to meaning stored in memory. For example, when you see a small-scale castle tower on a chess board, you understand that it is a chess rook, and therefore properly moves only along the board's ranks and files.

We use these three senses in making judgements, but what criterion should you use with them to make such judgements? The answer is *appropriateness*, which through inappropriateness, is illustrated in figure 4.17.

APPROPRIATENESS
Roger Scruton's *The Aesthetics of Architecture* fleshes the concept of appropriateness:[4]

1. The search for appropriateness is the search for an organizing principle, for an order implicit in the proportions and details. It leads automatically to the development of style.
2. Appropriateness is achieved when the existence of one part provides a reason for the existence of another.
3. Appropriateness is the natural fittingness of part to part, of an achieved articulation. . . . The correspondence of part with part is also a correspondence of the completed design with the designer and with those who will experience it.
4. Although appropriateness is a concept which cannot be defined, it can be demonstrated.
5. Appropriateness is not only an aesthetic concept, it can be applied to cost, function, meaning, etc.

When designing chess equipment, you should not only be seeking appropriateness within a single man; the men within a set are also parts of that set; and the set is in turn only part of the equipment involved in a game of chess. The concept of appropriateness in chess equipment is thus multilayered.

Although the clarification and realization of aesthetic intentions are an important part of designing, chessmen, at least in playing sets, have to communicate definite information to players.

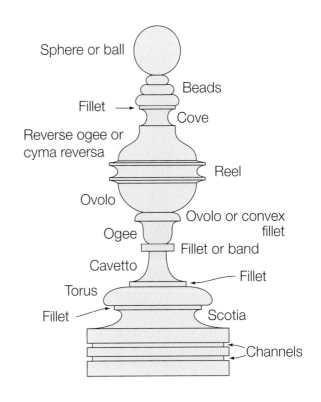

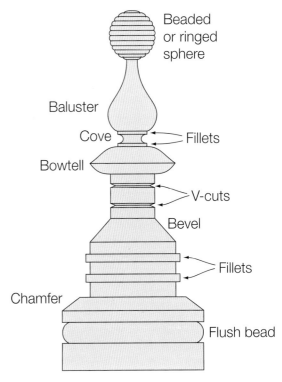

Figure 4.14 Pawn elevations illustrating the profiles of common named moldings. Fuller details of moldings are given in *Woodturning Design*, chapter 6.

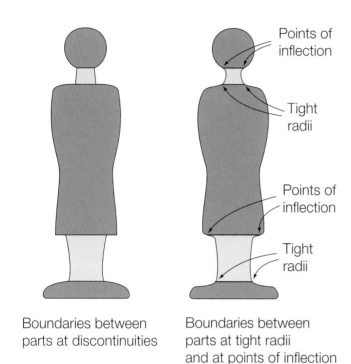

Boundaries between parts at discontinuities

Boundaries between parts at tight radii and at points of inflection

Figure 4.15 Boundaries where there are no discontinuities. *Left*, boundaries between parts are usually along surface discontinuities. *Right*, the concept of parts can still be applied to forms which have few if any discontinuities by implying boundaries at points of inflection or where there are tight radii.

Boundaries between parts may also be signified or reinforced by changes in material or decoration.

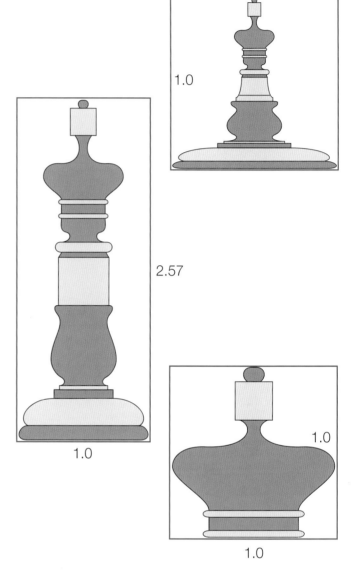

Figure 4.16 The influence of proportion. *Left*, the height:maximum-diameter ratio of the king from figure 4.13 is 2.57:1. *Right*, if you revise the ratio to 1:1 and wish the revised king to still be beautiful, you can radically change the proportions of the original parts (*top right*), eliminate some parts and modify the proportions of those retained (*bottom right*), or start a more radical redesign.

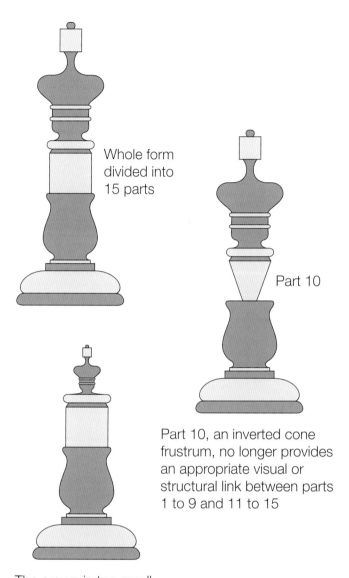

Whole form divided into 15 parts

Part 10

Part 10, an inverted cone frustrum, no longer provides an appropriate visual or structural link between parts 1 to 9 and 11 to 15

The crown is too small

Figure 4.17 The appropriateness and inappropriateness of part-groups and parts. *Top left*, the sizes, shapes, and meetings of parts and details in the original design are an appropriate manifestation of what we assume were the original designer's intentions. *Right center* and *bottom left*, just two of the infinite number of inappropriate versions of the original king.

You may be able to judge that there is inappropriateness and identify its source; for example, by saying that the crown part-group of the king, *bottom left*, is too small. You may not be able to explain why that smallness is inappropriate, but that does not undermine the validity of your aesthetic judgement.

4.3.5 COMMUNICATIVE INTENTIONS

When designing a playing chess set you should intend that each chessman in the set clearly communicates that it:

1. Belongs to that set.
2. Belongs to one of the two sides in that set.
3. Is a particular piece, a king, queen, bishop, knight, rook, or pawn.

Form, size, and color are the properties primarily used alone or in combination by chess-set designers to communicate that a man belongs to a particular

Figure 4.18 Confused piece signatures. Marcel Duchamp's king and queen both have crowns, but are the same height. Only because the ubiquitous Staunton design's king has an arched crown and its queen a pointed crown could you rightly conclude that the man on the left is Duchamp's king. The confusion would have been less had Duchamp's king been topped by a version of the Staunton king's orb and cross. This omission was Duchamp's "declaration of anticlericalism".[5]

set, belongs to the black or white side, and is a particular piece. Other properties such as surface texture, glossiness, and weight are usually less important communicators, but can confuse perceptions where not consistent through a set or not appropriate. When properties communicate set, side, and/or piece they are acting as what I call *signatures*. The most obvious signatures are the piece symbols discussed in the preceding chapter.

SIGNATURES
If you play with thirty-two men which seem to be from different sets, or if you are unclear to which side a man belongs, or which piece a man is (figure 4.18), you will be less able to concentrate on play and may mistake one man for another—hence the importance of clear signatures. Whether signatures are clear to players depends on what signatures are customary in that region at that time. Figure 4.19 illustrates my concept of signatures; it also demonstrates the need for signatures to be consistent through all the men of a set.

Figure 4.19 Confused set, side, and piece signatures. The Lopez design (men *E* to *K*), shown earlier in figure 2.13, was designed with clear signatures. If you analyze the signatures of men *B*, *C*, *D,* and *L*, and compare them with the Lopez mens' signatures, you will understand why men *B*, *C*, *D* and *L* cannot be Lopez men.

King *B*. Both body and crown are of the correct wood species for set and side signatures. The heights of the body and the crown are correct for the piece signatures, but the bulbous body form conflicts with the conic set signature. The carving to the top of the crown is contrary to the set signature of no carving, and the resulting pointed crown has become the customary piece symbol for the queen.

King *C*. All its innate signatures are correct except its size which is far too small to confirm set and piece.

King *D*. The ornament of the base cone and the wood species used for the cone do not conform to the expected set signatures. Similarly, the elaborateness of the crown and the wood species used for it do not conform to the expected set, side and piece signatures.

Pawn *L*. The absence of a sphere means that man *L* cannot belong to this Lopez set, but only because the sphere (or any other form of head) provides the wood species needed to give this man a side signature.

Signatures may be relative or absolute. Height is relative—the height of a man communicates little unless other pieces are present. A horse's head is an absolute piece signature because its presence allows a lone chessman to be identified as a particular piece (a knight) with certainty. A crown piece signature allows scope for conjecture—the man could be a king or a queen (figure 4.18). Number can be an absolute or a relative signature, and the certainty with which it communicates also depends on the number of men of the set present. If the full set is present and there are sixteen men with the same form, they must be pawns; similarly, if there are two men with the same particular form, they must be kings or queens.

4.3.6 MATERIAL, TECHNIQUE, AND EQUIPMENT INTENTIONS

A designer's intentions about form, weight, ornament, color, decoration, etc. usually dictate the materials, techniques, and equipment which will be employed by the set's maker. Particularly where the designer is also the maker, the maker can influence or dictate aspects of the design.

4.3.7 PERSONAL INTENTIONS

When you experience an object designed and made by others, your judgements are partially based upon your assumptions of the designer's and maker's intentions. If you are designing a chess set, and are concerned that those who later experience the set may make wrong assumptions about your design intentions and thus misjudge your design, you should try to ensure that a statement of your intentions accompanies the finished chess set. For example, someone may judge a chessman ugly, but suppose that it was made solely to practice a technique and was never intended to be beautiful. The judgement, while correct, is irrelevant because it is based on an understandable but false assumption.

4.3.8 THE IMPORTANCE OF INTENTIONS

Poor design often reflects a designer's lack of attention to intentions:

1. If you, the designer, define and grade your design intentions during the design process, your design is more likely to fulfill them.
2. If the designer's intentions and their relative importances are communicated to the maker, the maker will be better able to manifest the designer's vision accurately.
3. When defining intentions, is their acceptability to you the designer the only criterion? Should you attempt to assess how acceptable they might be to other likely experiencers, particularly the client or recipient? If others are likely to dislike the manifestation of your intentions, should you modify your intentions?

4.4 RESTRAINTS

Restraints are bars to intentions. If you attempt to list all the restraints which limit your freedom when designing an object, you will find that you had accepted many of them unconsciously. You can then decide which restraints from the list you will continue to accept, and which you will henceforth ignore.

An example of an unconscious restraint is that of unthinkingly designing the kings as the tallest men in a set. While a sensible restraint because it reflects what is customary, it need not be mandatory. Max Ernst made his queens taller than his kings because queens are more powerful in active play. There is also a case for making kings the shortest of the back-rank men because kings are moved less often than the other men, and because a player often has to reach over his or her king to move another man.

Another usually unconscious restraint is that turned chessmen must be symmetrical about a vertical axis—the key to my Lopez chess set (figure 2.13) was to design a knight which ignored that restraint.

4.5 PRELIMINARY DESIGN

Chessmen are relatively simple to design, and there is usually no clear separation between the preliminary and detailed design stages shown in figures 4.1 and 4.2. I shall therefore combine these two stages, and discuss their sum in section 4.7.

4.6 INITIAL DESIGN PROPOSAL

The initial design proposal is usually a formal document consisting of drawings (which may not be fully resolved), a specification, prices, a timetable, and contract terms including a procedure for settling disputes. The proposal should be sufficiently detailed to properly inform the client; and protect the designer, the maker, and the client from spurious claims.

4.7 DETAILED DESIGN

Because of the number and interdependence of the variables, you should finish designing a chess set before allowing its making to start. Figure 4.20 and this section describe the design process as if it were orderly and linear. It rarely is, and you will often have to backtrack to reassess or change an earlier decision, or you may progress in a different, even tortuous, order.

Your reason for designing is essentially to produce a design which fulfills your intentions for the chess set. You will greatly increase the probability of successful fulfillment if you apply the secret ingredient throughout the process. That ingredient is work, which consists of directed thought, trial and error, research, and interaction with others. Those with innate design talent have a design advantage, but they will not create consistently good designs without work. Equally, those who believe that they lack innate design talent can design extremely well if they are prepared to apply the effort. Most won't. Perhaps they don't realize that designing is just as enjoyable and rewarding as making.

Designing needs time. We cannot consciously reason forwards. We progress by applying *intuitions* (the conscious realizations resulting from subconscious mental processings). These processings have no set duration, and may take a fraction of a second, many

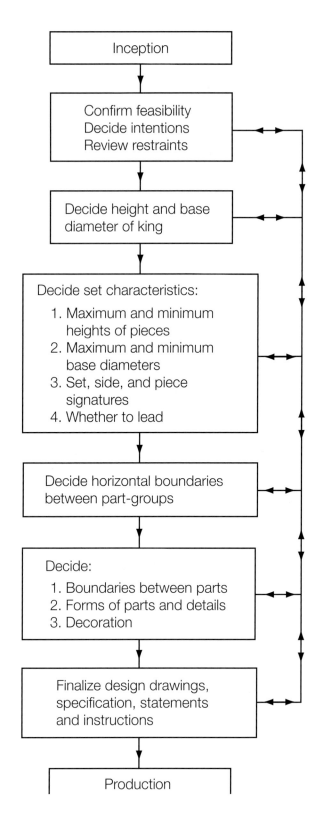

Figure 4.20 Designing a chess set, an idealized version of the process.

days, or longer. After we become conscious of an intuition, we can then attempt to judge its merit by reasoning. Both the intuition and the judgement of it are influenced by the information stored in memory—hence the importance of seeking knowledge.

4.7.1   DECIDE OVERALL DIMENSIONS

I will also assume that after clarifying intentions and restraints, your next step is to design the overall dimensions of the pieces, starting with the biggest, usually the king.

SIZE OF LARGEST PIECE
A king's maximum diameter is usually across its bottom, and is likely to be derived from, and will be between 50% and 80% of, the size of the squares on the intended board. The dimensions of the available pieces of woods you wish to use for the chessmen may also govern the maximum diameter.

You should next decide the king's overall height. Its magnitude will depend primarily on your intentions regarding stability, accessibility, and appearance, and may be influenced by what is customary.

Your next step is to decide how the overall heights and base diameters of the other five pieces should relate to those of the largest piece.

OVERALL HEIGHTS OF PIECES
The heights of the six pieces in non-travelling chess sets customarily differ, and are graded to aid piece identification (figures 4.21 to 4.23). However there is no particular grading of piece heights which is so dominant that it should be considered mandatory. In some sets, the tops of the six pieces lie on a straight, sloping line, but conformance is demanding because of the considerable variations in the heights of the customary Western piece symbols. You can design the heights of the back-rank men to form a symmetrical profile, but confusion will result unless you strongly differentiate the equally-tall king and queen by means other than height. Basing heights on the relative powers of the pieces in chess is initially tempting, but is impractical because the ratios of powers are as high as 9:1 (see page 69).

Figure 4.21   River sheoak copies of pieces with only slightly confused signatures which are analyzed in the next figure. The originals were made in England in the first half of the nineteenth century in unstained and red-stained ivory, and are pictured in Michael Mark, *British Chess Sets*, exhibit 27.

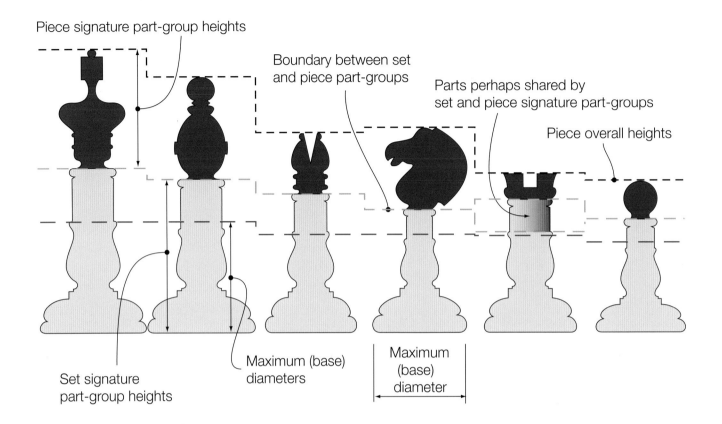

Figure 4.22 The part-groups and signatures of the pieces pictured in figure 4.21. The signatures are discussed below:

SET SIGNATURES
Readers will recognize that these six pieces belong to the same set because:

1. The pieces' total heights and base diameters lie within the customary ranges.
2. The set part-groups colored beige are all similar in form, and their heights and diameters lie within the customary range.
3. The six pieces are stylistically similar, and have similar dispositions of mass.
4. All the men of the original set were made in ivory.

SIDE SIGNATURE
The two original sides are differentiated only by organic and applied color.

PIECE SIGNATURES
1. The piece signature part-groups are clear to Western players, except perhaps that of the queen which has customarily had a spherical head rather than an ovoid one as here. The piece symbol for a pawn is also usually a sphere, but confusion is unlikely during play because pawns are customarily both smaller and less elaborately ornamented than queens, and because there are usually many more pawns on the board.
2. The relationships of the overall heights of the pieces are within the customary range.

BASE DIAMETERS OF PIECES

All piece base diameters are the same in some sets. In other sets the base diameters are usually reduced for shorter pieces, but usually vary less in magnitude than the piece heights. Ideally there should be a rationale for any reduction.

4.7.2 DECIDE SIGNATURES

Figures 4.21 to 4.28 demonstrate the three categories of signature. Set, side, or piece may each be signified by one signature or by a combination of signatures; for example, the crown and the overall height both signify the king in figures 4.21 to 4.23. Some features can also signify more than one of set, side, or piece. Thus in figure 4.26, the size and style of the graphics printed on the counters signify set, the graphics' colors signify side, and the subjects pictured by the graphics signify piece.

SET SIGNATURES

Set signatures are features which are common to every, or almost every, man in a set. These features include commonality of form, materials, ornament, style, workmanship, and decoration. That the sizes of all the pieces of a set lie within the customary range is also a set signature.

Figure 4.24 shows pieces with particularly complicated set-signature part-groups which also double as reinforcing piece signatures. In contrast, the disk-like forms of the men shown in figures 4.25 and 4.26 are unusual in that they do not contribute to piece identification.

SIDE SIGNATURES

You can communicated a man's side by color (either organic or applied), material, theme, size, and/or form. The employment of carving or modelling allows a wider choice of themes. Figure 4.35 shows the side signature of applied color reinforced by a small difference between the forms of the set-signature part-groups.

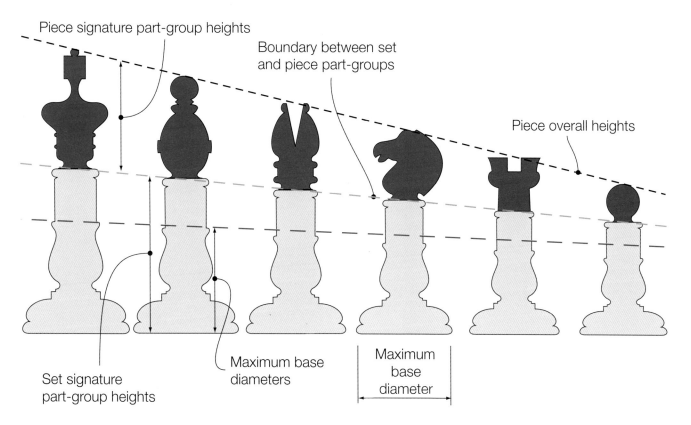

Figure 4.23 The pieces in the preceding figure "improved" by using more rational boundaries between part-groups. The diameters of the parts of the set signature part-groups have also been rationalized. The bishop is definitely better than the original, but the improvements to the knight and rook are less convincing.

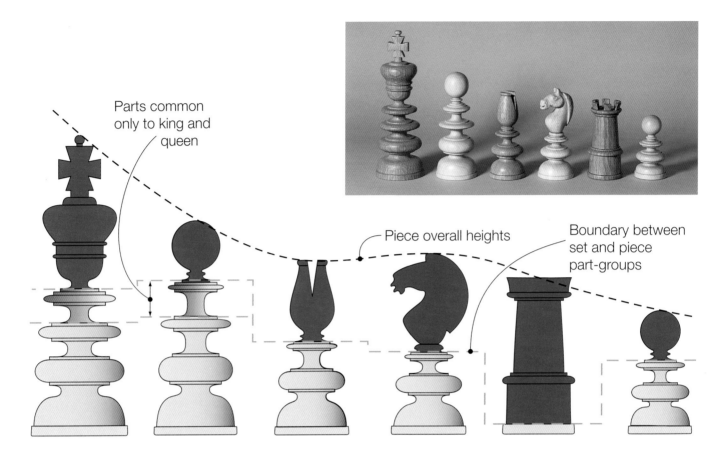

Figure 4.24 Copies of St. George pieces with signatures which are less rational than those shown in figures 4.22 and 4.23, but still clear. The design also has good playability and is aesthetically attractive.

SET SIGNATURES
1. The only part or part-group which is common to all pieces is the insignificant fillet at the bottom colored beige. The heights of these fillets are neither constant nor graded logically, but were probably intended to be the same.
2. All the pieces except the rook include similar set part-groups colored beige with a magenta tint on the right-hand side. The rook does not therefore strongly signify through its form that it belongs to this set.
3. The set part-groups of the king and queen have more parts than those of the bishop, knight, and pawn. The variations in the proportions and sizes of corresponding parts do not obey any formulae, but do not muddy piece identification because of the strong piece symbols.
4. The total heights and base diameters are within customary ranges.

SIDE SIGNATURE
1. The original side signatures are the organic colors of the ebony and boxwood used for the black and white sides respectively. The copies are in rock maple and English oak.

PIECE SIGNATURES
1. The magenta piece part-groups are customary in form but vary wildly in height; this makes designing the other parts of the pieces more demanding.
2. The relationships between the overall heights of the pieces are acceptably efficient piece signatures because they lie within the customary range.

PIECE SIGNATURES

Western sets usually have imitative piece-symbol signatures such as the crown of a king, or representative piece-symbol signatures like the sphere of a queen or a pawn. Forms which echo a piece's movement are also representative (figure 1.67). Piece signatures may also be geometric like those of Muslim sets, and be impossible for unfamiliar Western players to use (figure 4.27). The pieces shown in figure 4.28 have geometric piece signatures which only tenuously imitate the conventional Western piece symbols. The heights of the different pieces in a set commonly differ, but not all sets use this type of piece signature (figures 4.25 and 4.26).

As discussed earlier in subsection 4.3.5, a piece signature which does not need to be designed is the number of a piece in a set. However as not all the men of each piece are always on the board, it is desirable, though not essential, that a piece be identifiable in isolation.

Figure 4.26   A modern version of the set in the preceding figure, an inexpensive magnetic travelling set. The applied decorations supply both the side and piece signatures.

Figure 4.25   Ivory chessmen in the form of counters, made in China in the late nineteenth century for export to England. The major set signatures are the disk-like form and the carving style; the side signatures are organic and stained color; and the piece signatures are low-relief carved imitative and representative symbols.

Illustration courtesy of Garrick Coleman, London.

Figure 4.27   Pieces without imitative piece signatures, copies of Indian, eighteenth-century, Muslim, ivory chessmen. The original set is in the Gustavus A. Pfeiffer Collection in The Metropolitan Museum of Art, New York; it is pictured in *Chess; East and West, Past and Present*, by Charles K. Wilkinson and Jessie McNab Dennis, figure 10.

The set signatures are the banded-reel part-groups occupying about the bottom 80% of the height of each piece, and a similarity of size, style, and of decoration (the originals are ivory, with the one side stained red and the other green, and all men partially gilded).

The piece signatures are not imitative, but are the total form and height of each piece. The forms of the king and queen, and bishop and knight are almost identical except for the presence or absence of a small knop on top.

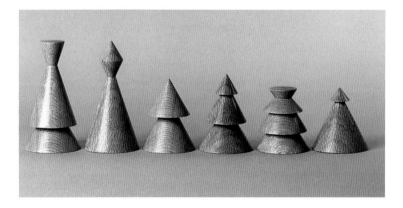

Figure 4.28   Confused piece signatures. Despite this set's abstract geometric style, the forms of its pieces vaguely imitate the forms of typical Western pieces such as those of the Staunton design. These silky oak (*Grevillea robusta*) pieces are copied from a Swedish set made about 1930 with one side in pewter, the other in brass. The original set is in the Gustavus A. Pfeiffer Collection in The Metropolitan Museum of Art, New York, and is pictured in *Chess; East and West, Past and Present*, by Charles K. Wilkinson and Jessie McNab Dennis, figure 106.

SET SIGNATURES
The main set signature is the theme of the cone. Other signatures are the use of polished metals, and all the pieces lying within the customary ranges of total heights and maximum diameters.

SIDE SIGNATURE
In the original set one side is turned from pewter, the other from brass. The side signatures are therefore based on organic color.

PIECE SIGNATURES
The Metropolitan Museum is uncertain which forms represent the bishop, knight, and rook. The right-hand piece is certainly a pawn because there are another fifteen men of similar form in the set. Because there are only two each of the two left-hand forms in the set, one must represent a king and one a queen, but which is which is not wholly certain, and is not further clarified by any difference between the overall heights.

4.7.3 DECIDE PART-GROUPS AND PARTS

When you decide that the forms of the men of a set should be more complicated than a counter, you will find that designing their forms to manifest your design intentions will be helped if you use the concepts of parts and part-groups.

DIVISION INTO PART-GROUPS

If you are designing in two dimensions, by deciding the piece heights and base diameters, you choose the dimensions of the enclosing rectangular frame for each piece (figure 4.29). If you are designing in three dimensions, the equivalent of the frame is a cylindrical container. Your next step is likely to be to divide these envelopes by horizontal planes to define the boundaries between your proposed part-groups. For clear communication of set, side, and piece, these boundaries should ideally coincide with the boundaries between signatures.

All the horizontal dividing planes may be positioned in the same proportional relationships in each piece (figure 4.23), but this desirable intention is often broken to a lesser or greater extent (figure 4.24). How high you position these horizontal planes within each piece should reflect the letter and the grading of your intentions, and the preferred form and dimensions of any set part-group or piece symbol. And although there aren't any rules for the heights of these planes which assure or maximize beauty, the guidelines first promoted by William Hogarth in his 1753 book *The Analysis of Beauty* have value, and are described in figures 4.29 to 4.31.

LEADING

If you decide that the men are to be leaded, you should design the amount of leading in each piece and decide the leading process. You should also ensure that the men's bases are capacious enough to hold the lead. Leaded chessmen usually have disks of baize or thin leather which hide the lead and allow the men to slide smoothly on the board.

DESIGNING PARTS

A part-group may be one part or a combination of parts. You decide the boundaries between the parts within a part-group in the same way that you decide the boundaries between the part-groups. You must also design the form and dimensions of each part at the same time because they will in turn influence the positioning of the boundaries between parts. Your sense of detail should be working hard during this process which is one of repeated trial and error. As you approach your final design, the scope of each adjustment should narrow. Be conscious, though, that a change in one part may suggest or require a revision not just to the adjacent parts, but also to more distant parts.

There are non-mandatory guidelines which relate to the design of parts, or more accurately details (figure 4.32), but, as figure 4.33 demonstrates, the process is one of successive refinement seeking appropriateness.

An aspect which influences appropriateness, and which you should therefore take into account when designing, is the angle from which players will typically view the men—there is little point in designing part-based signatures which cannot be seen during play.

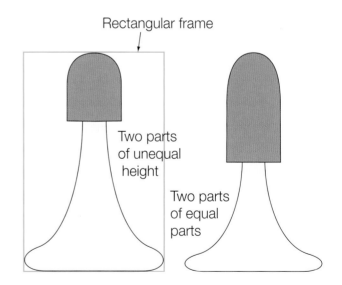

Figure 4.29 Pawns illustrating guideline 1. This guideline states that "when a form is divided by a horizontal into two parts and there is no overriding reason to make their heights equal, make their heights perceptibly unequal".

As predicted by guideline 1, the left-hand pawn is the more beautiful.

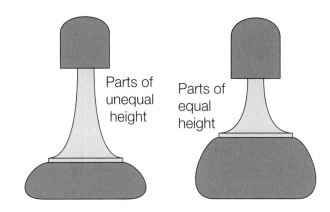

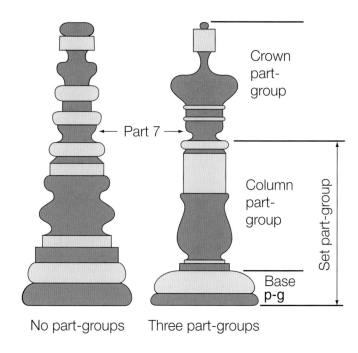

Part 7

Crown part-group

Column part-group

Set part-group

Base p-g

No part-groups   Three part-groups

Figure 4.30   Pawns illustrating guideline 2, which states "when a form is divided by horizontals into three parts and there is no overriding reason to make their heights equal, make their heights perceptibly unequal. The tallest part should be placed between the other two, or the parts should be arranged in order of part height with the shortest or tallest at the bottom".

As in the preceding figure, the left-hand pawn with unequal parts is more beautiful.

Figure 4.31   A demonstration of guidelines 3 and 4. These guidelines are

GUIDELINE 3

When a form can be divided by horizontals into more than three parts, the parts should first be combined into two or three parts and/or part-groups. After these have been designed using guidelines 1 and 2, the parts within the part-groups should be designed also using guidelines 1 and 2.

GUIDELINE 4

To avoid a top-heavy or unstable look, a form should usually decrease in width and depth (or in diameter) towards the top.

Both kings have 15 parts of similar shapes, and their parts are stacked in the same order. By varying the heights and shapes of the parts in the meaningless left-hand form, they have been made to coalesce into part-groups which make the right-hand form meaningful.

The cove in the joining part 7 beneath the crown and the expanded arched part of the crown reinforce the perception of a separate crown part-group.

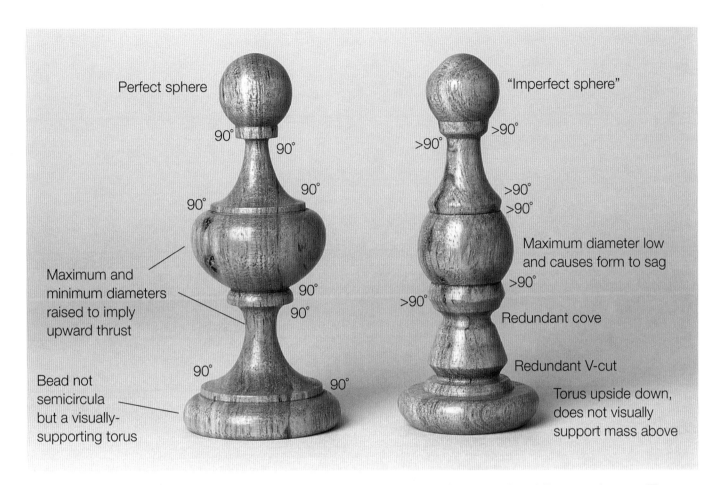

Figure 4.32 Guidelines for the preferred shapes, sizes, and boundaries of moldings and parts. The man on the left conforms to the guidelines, that on the right doesn't. The guidelines include:

1. Where appropriate, prefer strong changes in curvature and good contrasts in diameter.
2. Parts should not have forms which vaguely resemble geometrically defined forms. If, say, a part is intended to be a sphere, it should be truly spherical. If, as in the right-hand man, the top part is imperfectly spherical, it confuses and distracts a viewer. It confuses because the viewer is unsure whether the part was intended to be a sphere. It distracts because the viewer focusses on the top part's sphericity, and is therefore unlikely to focus on the man's more important features.
3. Details which confuse form or meaning should be deleted.
4. Fillets on an ogee curve should be placed at the points of inflection.
5. For maximum contrast, junctions between surfaces should be at 90° or 270°.
6. The forms of objects should confirm their structural roles. Chessmen are columns, albeit lightly loaded, and look better if their forms imply upward thrust and support.

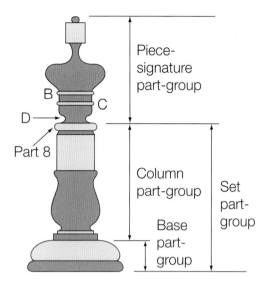

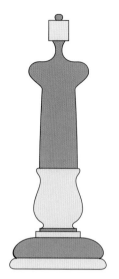

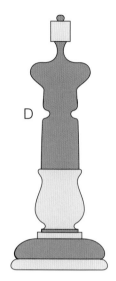

The tiny beads B and C imitate the fillets at the top and bottom margins of a crown's circlet. Cove D and part 8 articulate the separation between the piece and set part-groups

Eliminating B, C, D, and part 8 causes the crown part-group to become so tall that is barely recognizable, and to merge into the column part-group

Cove D alone helps to articulate the separation into crown and column, but is not definite enough, particularly when compared to the crispness of the rest of the form

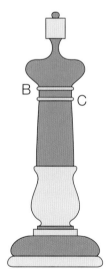

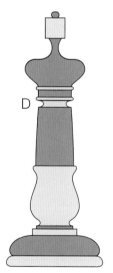

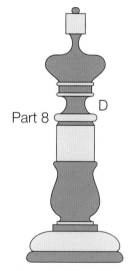

Introducing beads B and C alone does not provide enough separation between the crown and the column

Introducing the B, C, and cove D, but without the rest of what was part 7, gives better but still insufficient separation. The top of the column looks unfinished.

Enlarging cove D and adding bead part 8 gives improved separation. However I prefer the design of the original.

Figure 4.33 The importance of articulation, of the mutual support of meaning and form, for appropriateness in the designing of parts.

4.7.4 DECORATION

Decoration consists of surface colors and patterns, which may be organic and/or applied. The surface texture and the degree of glossiness, which result from the materials and workmanship which you specify as part of the design, are also decoration.

You can apply decoration with clear or tinted polishes, stains, dyes, paints, fabrics, and metal leaves. Decoration can be used to signify set, side, and/or piece. Decoration can be single-color and only signifying side (figure 4.35), or be more elaborate with patterns or designs, which may be imitative (figure 4.34). Take care that the decoration does not result in confused signatures. For wooden playing sets, a clear finish which sits on the surface is more likely to show damage than that which is largely absorbed into the surface. Materials which are not absorbent, such as ivory, bone and metals, are better not lacquered.

Form and decoration should be complementary; for example, the boundaries between different colors are especially clear when at the boundaries between parts.

Figure 4.34 Elaborate imitative decorations which clearly signify set and side. Because the decorations do not strongly imitate the customary Western piece symbols, and the forms of the men, except the queen, are similar, piece is signified by height.

This "Australian Pioneer" chess set was turned by Adrian Hunt, and designed and painted by Jilli Roberts, both of southern Tasmania. Adrian's "Deepings Dolls", named after his property, were pictured on page 101 of *Woodturning Design*. This set was inspired by the triptych painting "The Pioneer" by Frederick McCubbin (1885–1917). The kings are pioneers; the queens are pioneers' wives; the bishops are stockmen; the knights are troopers; the rooks are gold prospectors; and the pawns are homestead boys. Various Australian animals and birds are featured in the decorations. The colors of the two sides represent the summer and winter lights.

Figure 4.35   Simple decoration, black and white paints applied to a pale, plain, lightweight wood. This design was mass-produced in China in the 1990s. Although the set signature part-groups are similar in form for the black and white sides, those of the black side are slimmer.

Photographed courtesy of Mr. and Mrs. John Carroll.

4.8   SUMMARY

Designing a chess set is unlikely to follow the smooth linear process indicated by a superficial look at figure 4.20. Churning is the norm, and this inevitably involves revising and regrading choices made earlier. Fortunately you are not searching for one ideal solution because for any instance of intentions and restraints there are an infinite number of solutions which are economically, functionally, and aesthetically equivalent.

Some readers of this chapter will intend that their chess set designs should be perceived as art rather than as a "mere" chess sets. The essence of art is that it manifests an original idea. Originality is easier when there are fewer restraints. Abandon the restraint of playability and anything is possible, but what is the merit of the result as a chess set?

Originality is related to your ability to generate fresh associations of just-sensed input and knowledge you already hold in your memory. Those who are content to solve design problems by using solutions they already know will produce little that is original.

4.9   ENDNOTES

1. Eric Schiller, *The Official Rules of Chess* (New York: Cardoza Publishing, 2003), p. 35.

2. Roger Scruton, *The Aesthetics of Architecture* (Princeton, NJ: Princeton University Press, 1979), p. 223.

3. Roger Scruton, pp. 206–236.

4. Roger Scruton, pp. 222–232.

5. *The Art of Chess* (catalogue of the exhibition of the same name at Somerset House, London, held between 28 June and 28 September, 2003), p. 22.

Chapter Five

DRAWINGS FOR CHESS SETS

This chapter provides drawings of the pieces of my Lopez design and of the pieces of eight antique chess sets, seven of which were shown earlier in this book. I based my drawings of the antique sets on photographs, and on illustrations in books and journals. The resulting drawings may therefore not be absolutely accurate to the originals.

You may copy any of the designs exactly, modify them, or use them as a basis to create fresh designs. For example, figure 5.10 shows the pieces of an eightenth-century Russian set, and figure 5.11 shows a modified version with clearer piece signatures.

I have positioned the drawings towards the outside edge of the pages so that you can photocopy, scan, or trace more readily. You can scale the drawings up or down by using a scaling photocopier, or by other means. You can use your photocopy, print or tracing as a pencil gauge for all the pieces of a set by judicious folding (figure 5.1). The dark red, dashed lines on the drawings indicate where to fold to utilize the dark red reference lines. The blue grid has 5 mm squares.

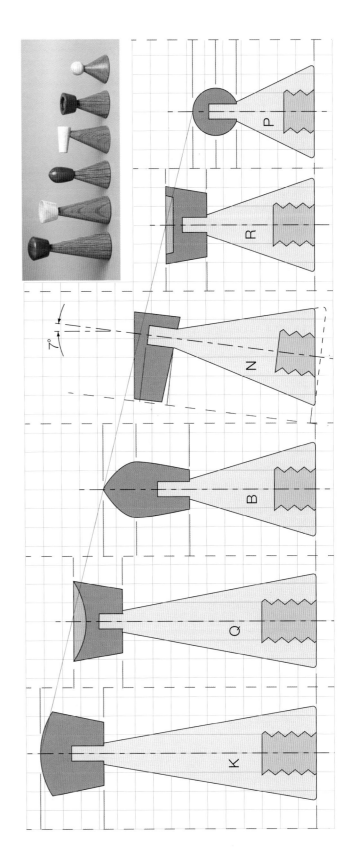

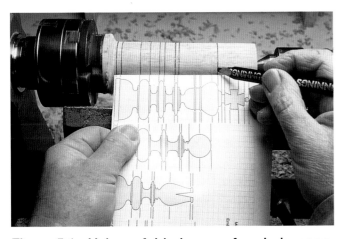

Figure 5.1 Using a folded copy of a whole-page drawing as a pencil gauge.

Figure 5.2 Piece designs for my Lopez design shown earlier in figure 2.13. All but the knight could be made in one piece.

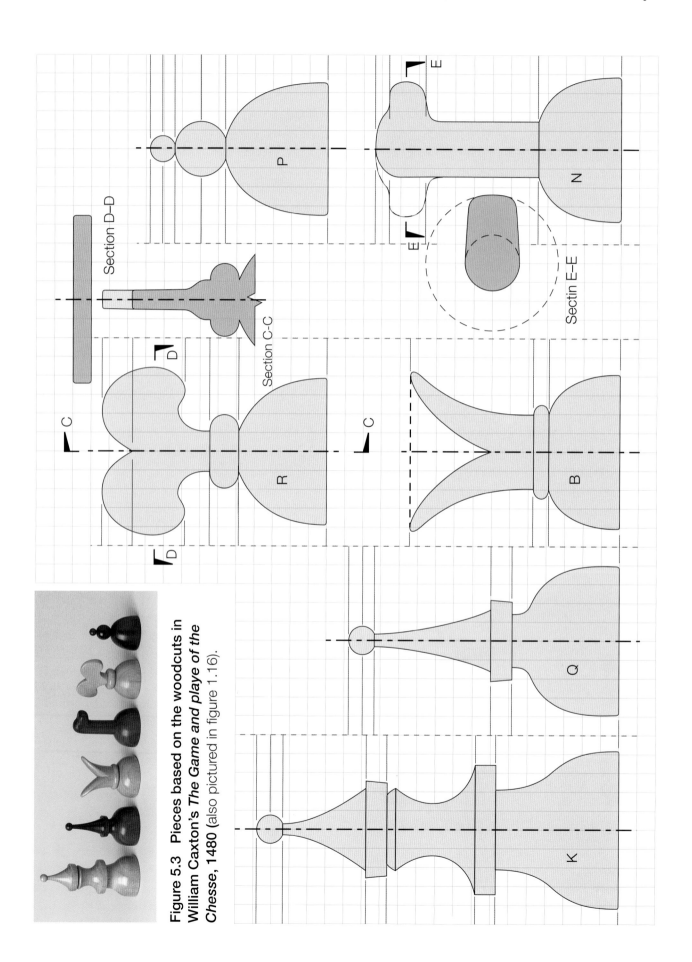

Figure 5.3 Pieces based on the woodcuts in William Caxton's *The Game and playe of the Chesse*, 1480 (also pictured in figure 1.16).

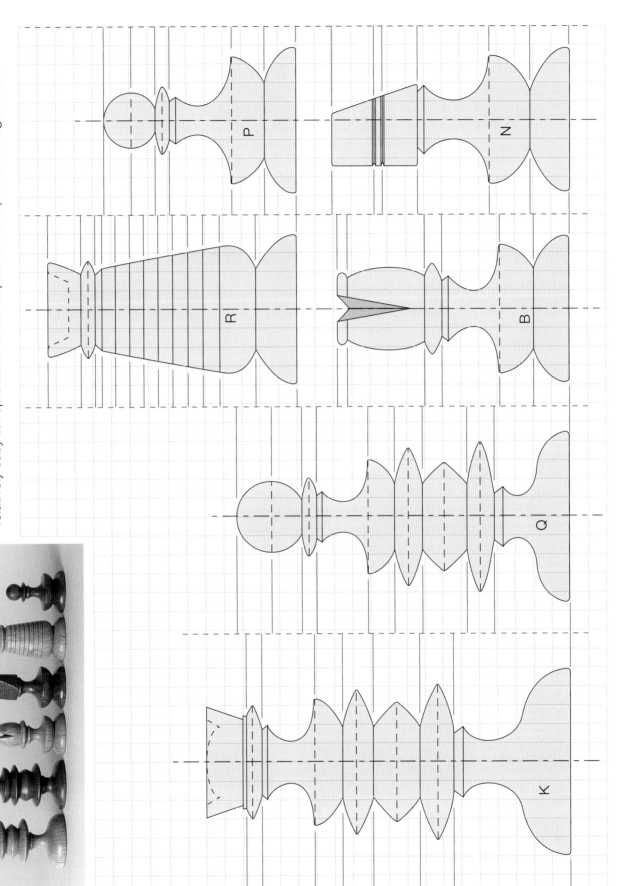

Figure 5.4 Copies of English wooden pieces made in the second half of the eighteenth century. The originals are pictured in Michael Mark, *British Chess Sets*, 2nd edition, 1996, exhibit 1. The cut-aslant knight makes the set relatively easy to reproduce. These copies are also pictured in figure 1.35.

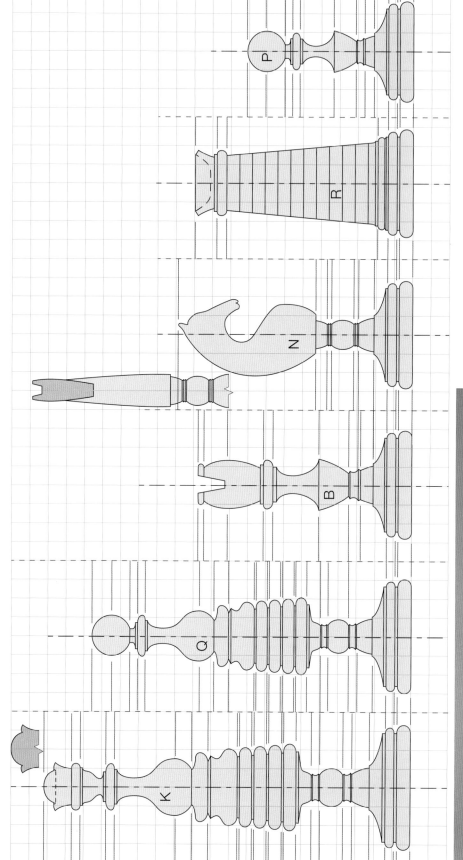

Figure 5.55 Copies of English-made barleycorn pieces based on pieces pictured in Gareth Williams, *Master Pieces*, pages 40 and 41.

The originals were made in about 1770 in ivory. I have therefore added a disk to the underside of the base of the ivory design to give the base sufficient strength to be serviceable in wood. These copies are also pictured in figure 1.36.

Note, the original rooks have imitation vertical joints between the ashlars.

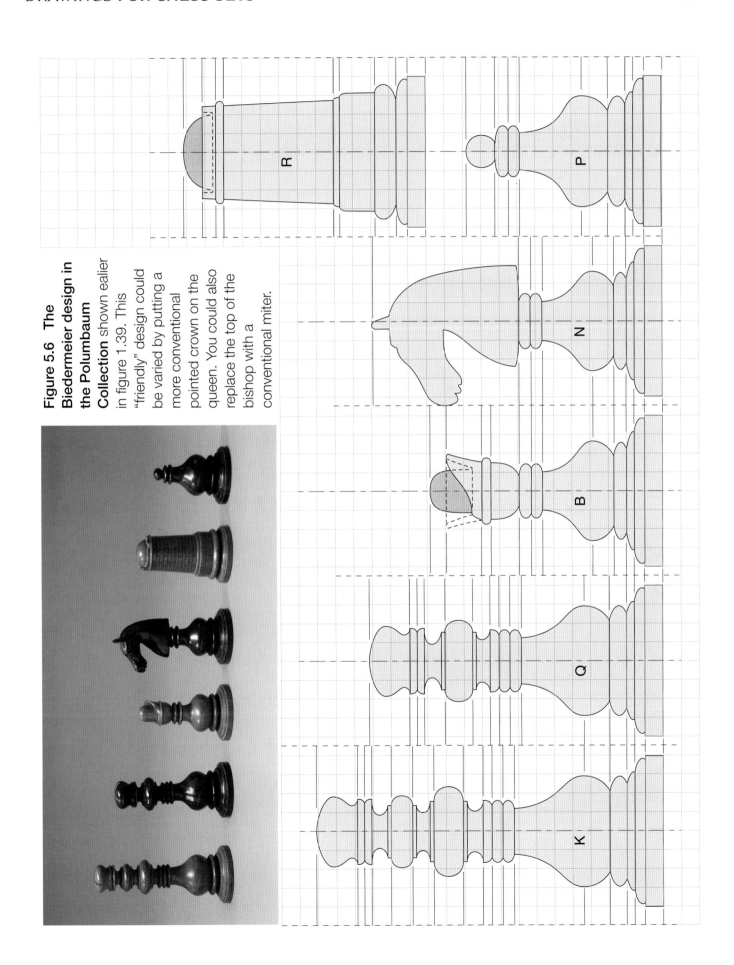

Figure 5.6 The Biedermeier design in the Polumbaum Collection shown ealier in figure 1.39. This "friendly" design could be varied by putting a more conventional pointed crown on the queen. You could also replace the top of the bishop with a conventional miter.

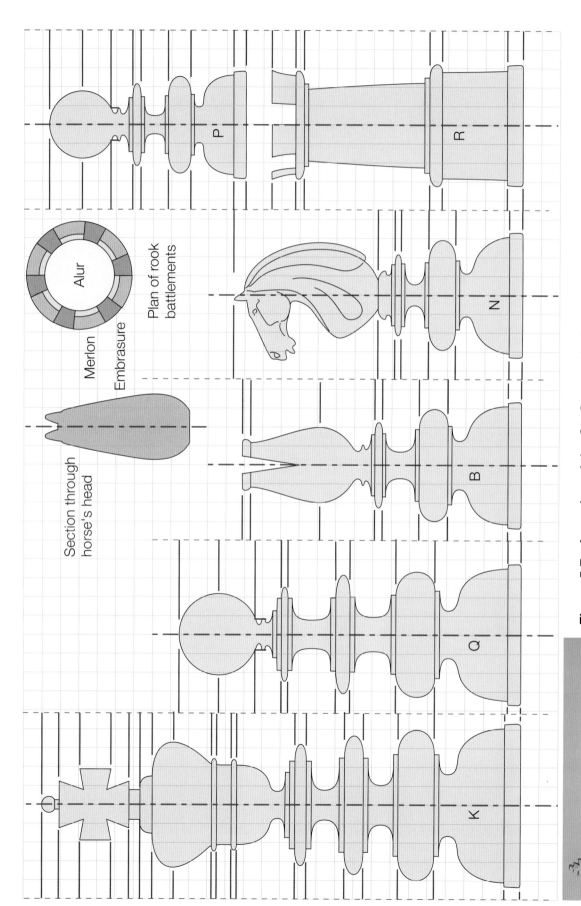

Merlon

Embrasure

Alur

Plan of rook
battlements

Section through
horse's head

P

R

N

B

Q

K

Figure 5.7 A version of the St. George design.
This design is analyzed in figure 4.24

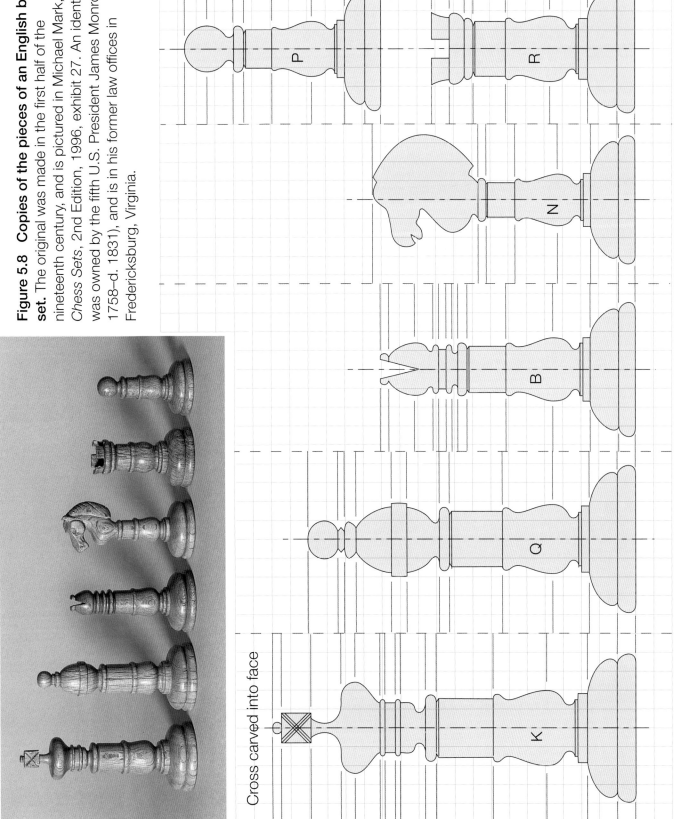

Figure 5.8 Copies of the pieces of an English bone set. The original was made in the first half of the nineteenth century, and is pictured in Michael Mark, *British Chess Sets*, 2nd Edition, 1996, exhibit 27. An identical set was owned by the fifth U.S. President James Monroe (b. 1758–d. 1831), and is in his former law offices in Fredericksburg, Virginia.

Cross carved into face

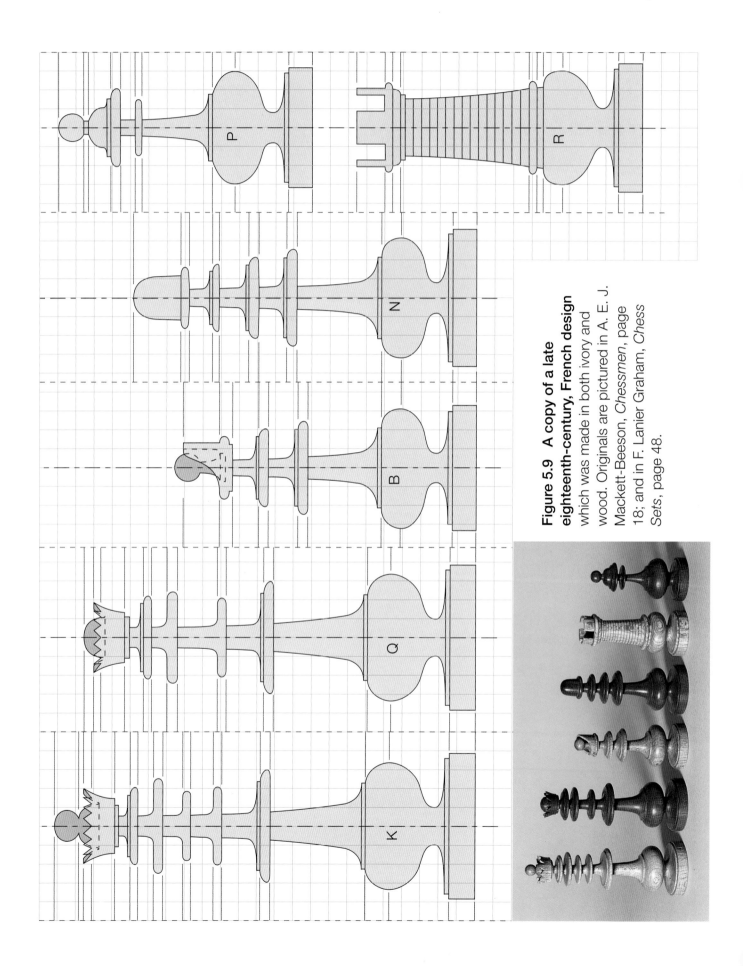

Figure 5.9   A copy of a late eighteenth-century, French design which was made in both ivory and wood. Originals are pictured in A. E. J. Mackett-Beeson, *Chessmen*, page 18; and in F. Lanier Graham, *Chess Sets*, page 48.

Figure 5.10 A copy of an elegant northern Russian, design. The original set was made in about 1800 in unstained and brown-stained bone, and is pictured in Gareth Williams, *Master Pieces*, pages 84 and 85. Note that the tops of the king, queen, and bishop are similar in form. These copies are in forest sheoak.

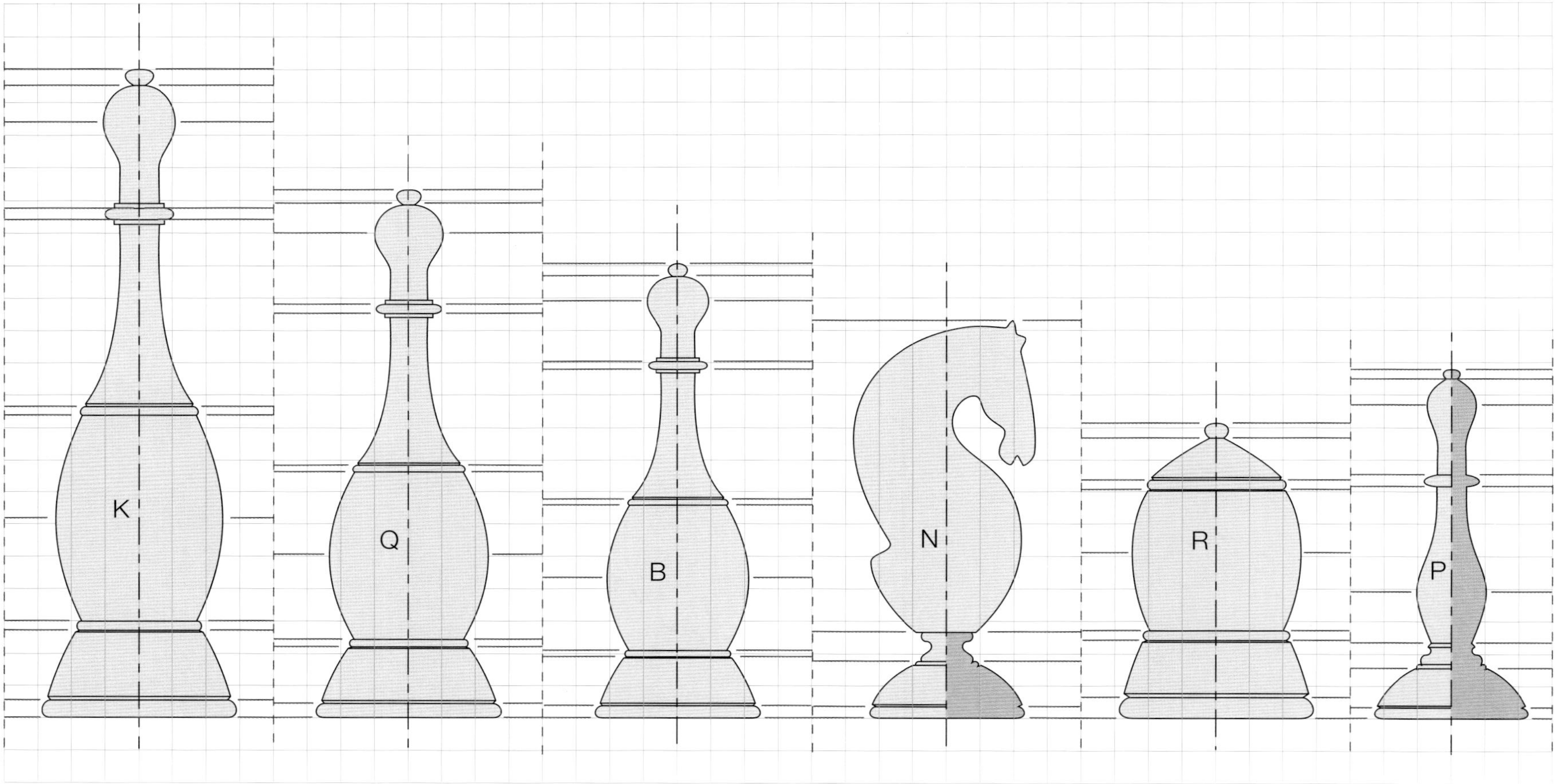

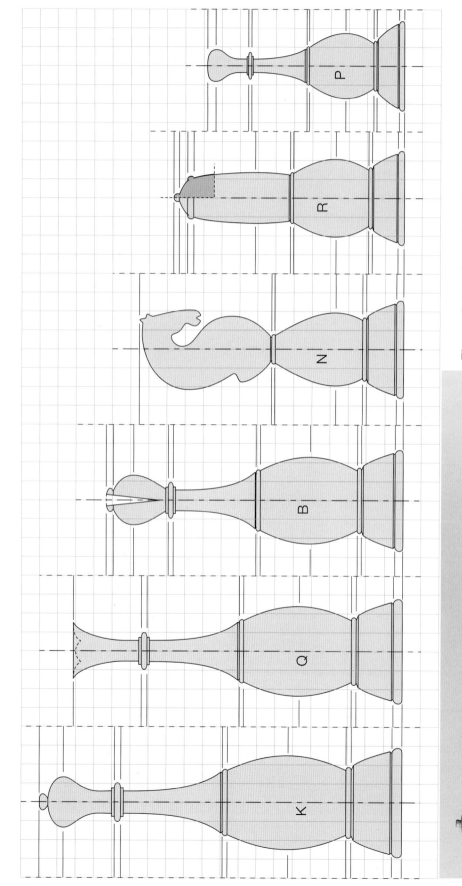

Figure 5.11   A version of the Russian design in the preceding figure 5.10 "improved" by applying Western piece signtures to the queen, and bishop; by retaining the essential form of the king, queen and bishop in the pawn; and by using the same ratios of part heights throughout all the pieces so that the tops lie on a straight, sloping line.

Chapter Six

MAKING CHESSMEN

In this chapter I discuss the materials, equipment, and techniques used to make turned wooden chessmen under thirteen headings:

1. Materials and their selection.
2. Turning and carving equipment.
3. Turning procedures.
4. Preparing turning blanks before mounting them in the lathe.
5. Roughing, which includes turning any features needed to chuck the blanks, and boring for leading.
6. Finish-turning.
7. Carving and special details.
8. Ornamenting and texturing.
9. Sanding.
10. Decoration and finishing.
11. Parting-off
12. Leading.
13. Baizing.

These techniques have changed little through the centuries, although leading and baizing may have been introduced and become common only relatively recently. You have, however, a surprisingly large number of choices in the order in which you can use the techniques, in the way you perform them, and in the equipment you can use for them. To describe all the choices would be tedious. I could describe only one procedure, but there is not one which is clearly superior. I have therefore opted to discuss the main alternatives, and where appropriate indicate their relative merits and my preferences.

Factory production of chess sets probably started in the second half of the eighteenth century. Automatic lathes started to displace hand turning for mass-produced sets from the end of the nineteenth century, by which time steam-engine-powered equipment was widely used by the major chess-set manufacturers as this description from *The Strand Magazine* of June 1895, found by Gareth Williams, demonstrates:[1]

> Perhaps the most important branch of work carried on in the immense turners' shop [at F. H. Ayres, 111 Aldergate Street, London] is the making of chess[men] . . . Sets of chess[men] are made of box-wood, rose wood, ebony, bone and animal and vegetable ivory; they range in price up to £20, and are sent to all classes in every part of the world, from Oriental monarchs to lonely Canadian settlers. In the manufacture of chess and draughts [chessmen and checkers], twenty men are regularly employed; and I stayed for a few moments to watch one of these who was carving [knights'] heads. The first tool he used was a circular saw; and with this he cut little bits from a big piece of rough ebony. He then mounted a toothed wheel 1.5" in diameter, set it revolving swiftly, and held one of the bits of ebony to it. Gradually one could see that by deft manipulation the familiar head was growing under the turner's hand; another and smaller wheel was presently mounted, and so on until the last circular saw had no greater diameter than the head of an average pin. There were seventeen changes of tools, but the entire process took no more than a quarter of an hour. An expert man can produce four dozen heads per day. Lest any of my readers should marvel at the mention of vegetable ivory, I hasten to explain that it a sort of solid Brazil [tagua] nut which is bought in sacks by the ton.

The Strand Magazine article also mentioned that 65,000 elephants were then being killed each year for their ivory, which was used mainly for billiard balls.

6.1 MATERIALS

Chessmen have been made from almost every solid material, including: wood, bamboo, stone, rock crystal, precious stones, jet and other semiprecious stones, ivory, bone, horn, vegetable "ivory", amber,[2] artificial resins and plastics, glass, porcelain, other ceramics, and metals. Chessmen have also been made from materials which lack solidity, including: vegetables, chocolate, papier mâché, cardboard, living bushes trained and trimmed into topiaries, and fibres. Then there are the virtual chessmen which appear as images on screens. However this chapter focuses on making chessmen from wood, and similarly-turnable materials such as ivory, bone, horn, and some resins and plastics.

6.1.1   WOOD SELECTION

Boxwood, ebony, and African blackwood have long been favored for chessmen. However, most woods can be used, with the harder, finer-grained species being better for men of typical size. Plainer woods are generally preferred for more intricately turned and carved men because there aren't any color patterns in the woods to confuse our perceptions of the forms.

Figure 6.1   A king turned from woods with striking colors, and a rook turned from a mulberry blank containing sapwood and heartwood. The king is turned from Osage orange and padauk. Six parallel holes were drilled into the padauk to imitate arches before its outside and inside were finish-turned.

Over time, bright wood-colors lose their intensity, and polishes will usually yellow, brown, or whiten.

Another factor which may influence your choice of a wood is its color or pattern of colors, particularly if you intend side signatures to be communicated by organic color (figure 6.1).

If you intend to shape men by scraping, as in ornamental turning, select from those species which scrape well. Similarly if your design requires carving, choose species which can be carved to the designed fineness of detail—if necessary try carving a sample.

You should ensure that you have sufficient wood for the set or for the side. You will need more wood if you intend to make a box, board, or other equipment from the same species. For color consistency prefer that all the blanks can be cut from the same piece of wood, or from pieces from the same tree. You should also decide whether only heartwood can be used, and if "no", whether the sapwood feature will be used as a signature, or just decoratively (figure 6.1). Include in your wood requirement an allowance for making extra men or components to replace those which are not correctly made or are spoilt by flaws in the wood, and for making spare men. The wood should be seasoned to avoid degrade occurring in the completed men, and to avoid eruptions if you intend to lead with molten lead. Fortunately, for a set of chessmen of typical size, the required quantities of seasoned woods free of pith and degrade are still usually readily available.

6.2   WOODTURNING AND CARVING EQUIPMENT

This section discusses the woodworking, woodturning, and carving equipment you may need.

You should be able to prepare turning blanks more efficiently if you have a well-equipped woodworking workshop with say a planer, thicknesser, sawbench, bandsaw, horizontal borer or drilling machine, and a range of other woodworking tools and equipment. You can also prepare turning blanks with only a hand saw for crosscutting, and a hammer and steel wedge for riving along the grain.

However you have prepared your turning blanks, you will need equipment for the detailed shaping and other operations required to produce a chess set. I discuss this equipment below.

LATHES

Almost any woodturning lathe will do for turning chessmen between centers. You will need a robust headstock and bed if you intend to turn men from workpieces cantilevered from a chuck. (I will use the term *cupchucked* to refer to a workpiece held in this way, although several different chuck types and even the headstock spindle swallow can be used to cupchuck a workpiece). You don't have to use a small or miniature lathe (I much prefer a standard-sized lathe), but if you do, get a long-enough toolrest—most of those supplied as standard on miniature lathes are too short. An indexing facility is especially useful, in part because it doubles as a headstock-spindle lock, necessary when marking out and when sawing or carving. Where you do not have an indexing facility or it cannot provide the number of divisions you need, you can make a supplementary facility (figure 6.2).

Chessmen are typically small and ornate, and are therefore better and more efficiently finished when mounted in or on the lathe. Being able to quickly change lathe speed is an advantage, and therefore electronic speed variation is valuable, but not essential. The ability to change lathe speed quickly is also useful for boring.

Good illumination is essential for turning and carving chessmen. I have supplemented my overhead fluorescent fittings with an adjustable lamp (figure 6.2).

CHUCKS AND JIGS

You can use any of the manufactured chuck types shown in figure 6.4 to cupchuck chessmen. You will need a drill (Jacobs) chuck on a Morse-taper arbor for boring. A drive center is also a chuck, and you may need a smallish one, plus a live, preferably cone, tail center. You may also need to make special-purpose chucks, such as the tap chuck in figure 6.3, and jigs to use with your lathe or with other machines such as a table saw, and these are discussed in the sections in which they are shown being used.

HAND WOODTURNING TOOLS

You may need to supplement your present range of woodturning tools with smaller skews, gouges, and scrapers, depending on the forms and sizes of the men you intend to turn (figures 6.5 to 6.7). If there are cutting tools which you will use mainly for turning chessmen,

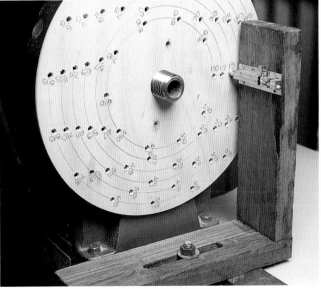

Figure 6.2 A supplementary inboard indexing facility—a similar arrangement could be mounted at the left-hand end of any suitable headstock. Here circles of 10, 7, 9 ,11, 13, and 15 equally-spaced holes have been drilled through the plywood dividing plate. The plate is locked onto the spindle when the chuck is screwed on. The index is a simple bolt.

you should consider reducing their sharpening angles to 5° less than normal. Ensure that your tools' blades are stiff enough not to flex noticeably during use.

CARVING TOOLS

The range you need is obviously related to the sizes of the features you have to carve, but will typically include a selection of small chisels and gouges, and perhaps a veiner (figures 6.8 and 6.9). If you use rotary carving heads with burrs, you'll find that they tend to leave a damaged surface and subsurface which you cannot quickly sand away.

SUNDRY EQUIPMENT

You will need calipers, preferably vernier, appropriately-sized drills, a rip hand saw, and finishing equipment including a small brush.

Figure 6.4 Manufactured chucks suitable for turning chessmen. *B* is a Oneway Screw Chuck. Its arbor is internally threaded at its smaller end to take a drawbar so that the chuck does not rattle out of the headstock-spindle swallow. *C* is a scroll chuck (a Oneway Talon chuck); *D* is a Craft Supplies collet chuck; *E* is a Glaser-type screwchuck made by Vicmarc; and *F* is a cupchuck made by Woodfast.

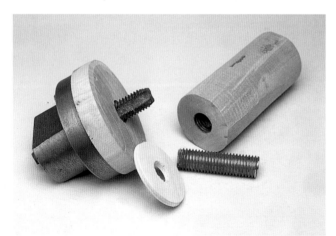

Figure 6.3 A homemade tap chuck used for workpieces which have been bored for leading. The small faceplate has been bored and tapped to the $^5/_8$ in. BSW thread of the hand bottoming tap. The tap was then locked into the faceplate with a nut. A wood cover plate with a slightly concave front face was then screwed onto the faceplate.

For this size of tap, a $^9/_{16}$ in. or 15 mm diameter hole should be bored into the workpiece. When screwing the workpiece onto the tap chuck, use the tailstock to keep the workpiece axially aligned. Each time you remount a workpiece on a tap chuck, the tap will tend to destroy more of the wooden thread. Replacing the tap with a length of threaded rod (here cut off a machine screw) will allow the workpiece to be securely remounted more times.

An advantage of this chuck is that the thread left in the wood will hold the leading securely, which obviates any need for undercutting.

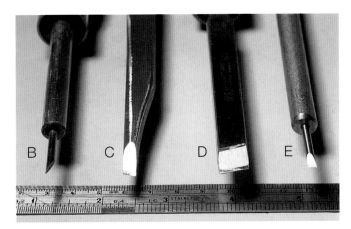

Figure 6.5   Small turning chisels: *B*, $^1/_8$ in. (3 mm) HSS rod skew (or is it a gouge?) for turning deep, narrow coves; *C*, a skew ground from 12.5 x 6.25 mm stock; *D*, a skew with an 11.5 x 5 mm blade cross section; and *E*, a skew ground from $^1/_8$ in. (3 mm) diameter HSS.

Figure 6.7   Small, straight scrapers: *B*, for undercutting for leading (see figure 6.24); *C*, for between the points and caps of crowns; *D*, ground from a worn-down gouge; *E*, for scraping alurs; *F*, ground from a broken tap.

Figure 6.6   Small gouges for spindle turning. *Left*, a 6 mm diameter bowl gouge with its flanges ground down and its nose ground to a detail gouge form; *right*, an 8 mm diameter detail gouge. Below, a narrow Norton slipstone suitable for honing small-fluted gouges.

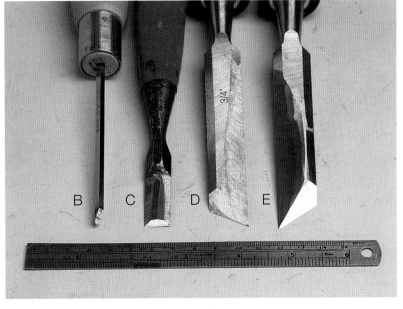

Figure 6.8   Carving chisels. *B*, a chisel ground from 1/8 in. (3 mm) square HSS. The other three chisels are ground from bevel-edged cabinetmakers chisels.

Figure 6.9   Carving tools and vernier calipers. The two carving gouges on the left are ground from worn woodturning detail gouges. The V-shaped tool, third from the left, is a veiner.

6.3   METHODS FOR TURNING CHESSMEN

You can chuck and turn a turned chessman in many different ways. The main routes from blank to completed chessman are described in figure 6.10. Corresponding chucking methods are outlined in figures 6.11 and 6.12. None is clearly superior. What factors should influence your choice?

1. I prefer to cupchuck the workpieces for rooks and all chessmen which have concave or recessed tops. The outer section of an unusually-large circular alur can be turned out between centers with a special scraper leaving only a central section of waste which can readily be trimmed away by hand, but such large alurs are rare.
2. Men with convex or flat tops are most quickly turned between centers. My preference is to have the bottom of a man at the tailstock end. As finishing (applying stains, polishes, etc.) is best done in the lathe, delay trimming off the waste spigot, local sanding, and patch finishing until the main finishing is completed.
3. If the material for a man is costly, you may prefer to eliminate the need for chucking spigot by

mounting the workpieces between centers, or on a screwchuck or tap chuck.
4. Unless there is a significant penalty, use the same chucking method for all the men of a set.
5. If a man is to be made from components, those which have to be bored are best cupchucked so that they can be accurately bored in the lathe.
6. You will not easily be able to clamp a finish-turned chessman and bore it for leading without damaging its surface. If a man is to be leaded, should you bore the hole for the lead in the lathe or not? Does the hole need to be undercut before the man is finish-turned?
7. If you need to carve all or part of a man, should you make the man in one piece, or in pieces which are later glued or screwed together? Will the carving be easier if the workpiece is held in a chuck? To hold the workpiece while you carve it, do you need to allow extra waste?
8. The equipment you have, or are prepared to make, buy, or modify.

Which chucking method do I prefer? I favor a tap chuck for men which are to be leaded. For unleaded men I favor a small scroll chuck. But I stress again that the differences between different methods are marginal.

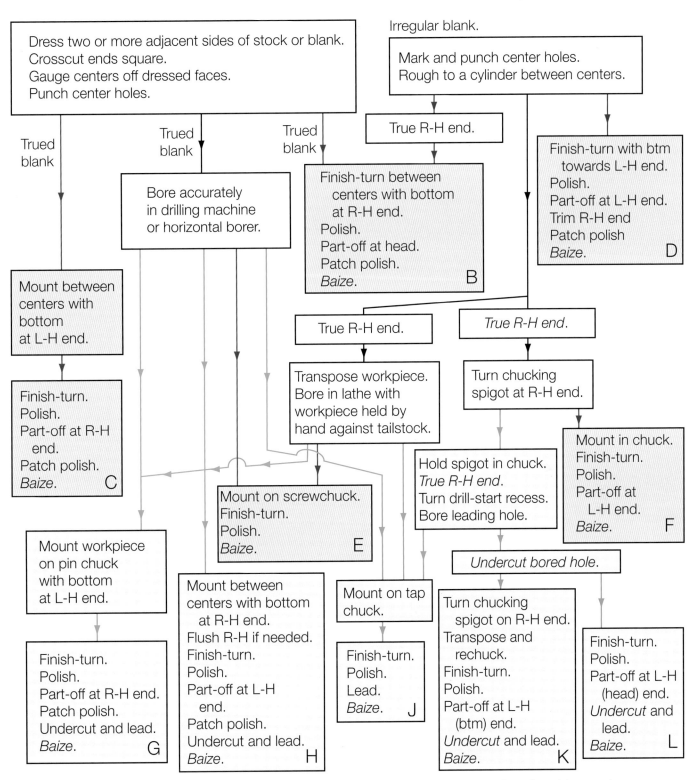

Figure 6.10 A flow chart showing the main choices for preparing the wood and making a chessman. The yellow boxes and black lines apply whether the man is to be leaded or not; the blue boxes and blue lines apply to a leaded man; and the red boxes and red lines apply to an unleaded man. The letters in the bottom right-hand corners of the boxes at the ends of paths refer to illustrations in the next two figures. An operation written in italics is optional. The finish-turn operation includes sanding. The patch polish operation includes any local sanding.

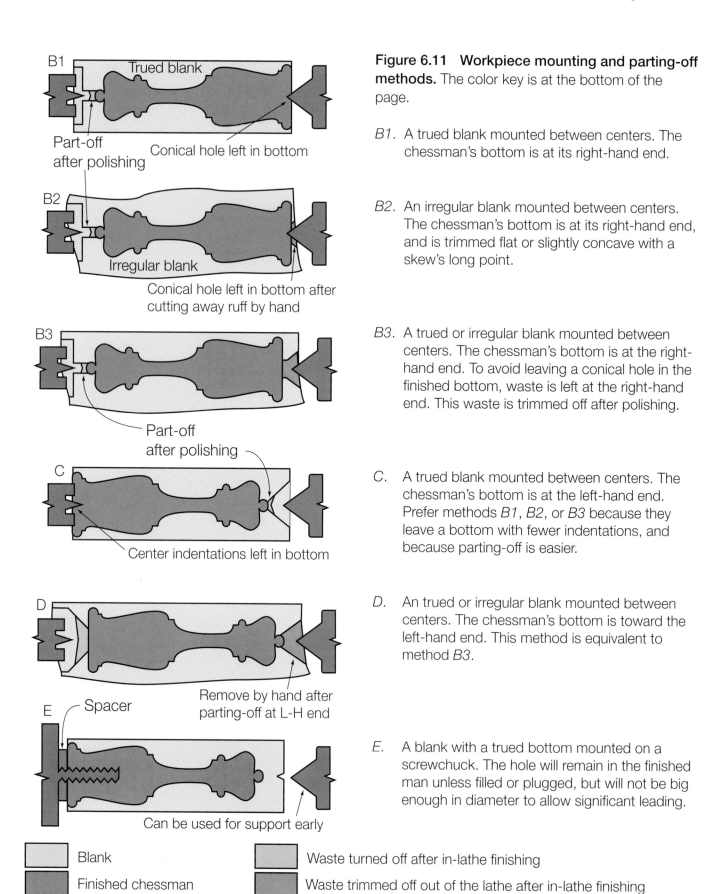

Figure 6.11 Workpiece mounting and parting-off methods. The color key is at the bottom of the page.

B1. A trued blank mounted between centers. The chessman's bottom is at its right-hand end.

B2. An irregular blank mounted between centers. The chessman's bottom is at its right-hand end, and is trimmed flat or slightly concave with a skew's long point.

B3. A trued or irregular blank mounted between centers. The chessman's bottom is at the right-hand end. To avoid leaving a conical hole in the finished bottom, waste is left at the right-hand end. This waste is trimmed off after polishing.

C. A trued blank mounted between centers. The chessman's bottom is at the left-hand end. Prefer methods B1, B2, or B3 because they leave a bottom with fewer indentations, and because parting-off is easier.

D. An trued or irregular blank mounted between centers. The chessman's bottom is toward the left-hand end. This method is equivalent to method B3.

E. A blank with a trued bottom mounted on a screwchuck. The hole will remain in the finished man unless filled or plugged, but will not be big enough in diameter to allow significant leading.

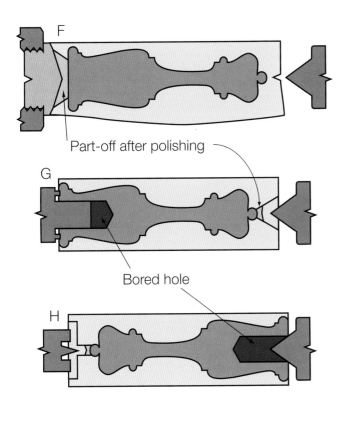

Part-off after polishing

Bored hole

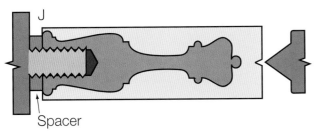

Spacer

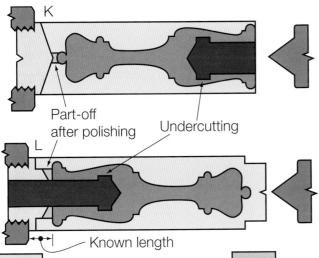

Part-off after polishing

Undercutting

Known length

	Blank		Waste turned off after in-lathe finishing
	Finished chessman		Waste trimmed off out of the lathe after in-lathe finishing
	Waste left on to allow wood to be rechucked for finishing		

Figure 6.12 More mounting and parting-off methods.

F. A trued or irregular blank mounted in an outside-gripping scroll or collet chuck, a screw cupchuck, or a cupchuck. The tailstock may be used to provide early support.

G. A prebored blank with a trued left-hand end mounted between centers and driven by a pin chuck or similar. You could use the central pin of the chuck to drive the workpiece if it was longer than the bored hole.

H. A prebored blank with a trued bottom mounted between centers. The chessman's bottom is at the right-hand end.

J. A blank with a trued, bored bottom mounted on a tap chuck. The spacer should be as large in diameter as possible and thick enough to allow tool access to roll the adjacent torus.

K. A blank with its bottom at the right-hand end. After boring, and any undercutting, it is advisable to use the tailstock to provide support.

L. A trued, bored, undercut-or-not blank cantilevered from an outside-gripping chuck. For undercutting, the blank must have earlier been cantilevered from a chuck gripping its right-hand end as in *K* above. Use tailstock support as needed. Mark out from the face of the chuck to ensure that the correct length of bored hole is retained for leading

6.4 PREPARING BLANKS FOR TURNING

If you take care when marking the centers, a blank's minimum thickness need only be 1/8 in. (3 mm) greater than the maximum finished diameter of the man. If you intend to use a chuck which grips onto a waste spigot, the minimum spigot size which your chuck can grip may determine your blank's minimum diameter. The lengths of waste you need to leave at each end of a blank depend on the design of the man, and on how the blank will be chucked, which can be judged from figures 6.11 and 6.12. You can lessen the minimum waste lengths if the center pin of your driving center does not project unnecessarily far past the edges of the driving prongs, and by using a cup tail center instead of a cone tail center. However, a cone tail center is better when its imprint will be used to center a drill for boring, and when finish-turning a man between centers with its bottom to the right.

The blanks for individual men are ideally crosscut from a long, straight-and-axially-grained pieces of wood of square cross section, but blanks with irregular cross sections and irregular ends are also entirely suitable.

BLANKS FOR TURNING BETWEEN CENTERS
A *trued* blank has two adjacent flat sides at 90° to one another; ends crosscut smooth, flat and perpendicular to the two sides; the turning centers gauged from the two sides and punched; and, if required, a hole bored along its turning-axis outside the lathe. If mounted carefully between centers, either end of a trued blank can be the finished bottom of a chessman; if mounted on a screwchuck or tap chuck, the bottom end does not first need to be skimmed in the lathe.

6.5 ROUGHING BLANKS

Roughing is a confusing term to because it is involves smoothing the blank, not making it rougher, and with a roughing, not a smoothing, gouge. Here *roughing* means 'preparing the blank in the lathe for finish-turning', and may comprise up to four of the five roughing operations described in this section.

LATHE SPEED
Chessman blanks of about 2 in. (50 mm) diameter can be roughed and finish-turned at up to 3000 rpm, but much lower speeds work well, and should be preferred when the workpiece is held in a heavy chuck, is irregular, or is slender. Your lathe's speed may also need to be reduced for boring and for finishing.

6.5.1 MOUNTING AND INITIAL ROUGHING

You will mount an irregular blank more evenly if you first eye and punch conical recesses in the blank's ends to locate on the points of your lathe's drive and tail centers (figure 6.13). You should also consider punching center recesses into the ends of trued blanks after gauging the centers. The next operation is to rough the blank to a cylinder (figure 6.14).

Figure 6.13 Punching conical recesses "by eye" into the centers of the ends of an irregular blank.

Figure 6.14 Roughing the blank to a cylinder of diameter somewhat bigger than the either the maximum finished diameter of the chessman or the minimum diameter required by your outside-gripping chuck.

Figure 6.15 Squaring the right-hand end of the workpiece with a roughing gouge. You could also use a parting tool, or the long point of a skew with its lower face flat on the toolrest.

Perform this cut before you bring the workpiece to the finished maximum diameter of the chessman because it tends to tear out fibers from the cylinder's surface. This cut is only necessary if the end of the blank is very uneven, otherwise square the end directly as shown in the next figure 6.16.

6.5.2 TRUING THE RIGHT-HAND END

You will need to true the right-hand end of a workpiece if that end will be the finished bottom of the chessman, or to maximize the effective length of a chucking spigot. You will usually only need to use the second of the two types of cut shown in figures 6.15 and 6.16.

Figure 6.16 Cutting the end of the blank flat or slightly concave with a skew's long point.

6.5.3   TURNING A CHUCKING SPIGOT

You should prefer to turn a chucking spigot on a workpiece which you will hold in an adjustable outside-gripping chuck because the shoulder if cut cleanly should align the workpiece axially. Such spigots may be required for finish-turning an unleaded chessman, for a workpiece for boring, or for a workpiece which is already chucked and is about to be or just has been bored. Most chucking spigots should be cylindrical or dovetail-sectioned, and have an appropriate diameter and length. For chucks such as a cupchuck or the headstock-spindle swallow, the spigot will need to be turned to a particular taper. Chucking spigots are usually turned on the right-hand ends of the workpieces.

If the chucking spigot's diameter is only a little less than the workpiece's, you need not rough the spigot first as in figure 6.17. You should still however cut a clean, precise spigot and shoulder as shown in figures 6.18 and 6.19 because the workpiece will then tend to be gripped more axially in the chuck, and the chuck will hold more securely. Further, if the workpiece has to be chucked several times, a chuck with radially movable, outside-gripping jaws should grip the workpiece identically at each rechucking if you insert the workpiece into the chuck in the same orientation. For this you need to pencil a reference mark onto the workpiece as described in figure 6.40.

Figure 6.18   Truing the radial face of the chucking spigot's shoulder with a skew.

Figure 6.17   Roughing a chucking spigot with the left-hand corner of a roughing gouge. This is a *cutting* cut, not a scrape. Note the prototype of the chessman mounted in the sanding rack for easy reference while finish-turning. The sanding rack is shown more fully in fgure 6.86.

Figure 6.19   Truing the cylindrical surface of the chucking spigot. The finish-turning of this workpiece is shown in figures 6.40 to 6.47.

6.5.4 BORING A HAND-HELD WORKPIECE

Chessman workpieces need to be bored for mounting on a small-diameter screwchuck, or if they are to be leaded. You should consider sizing the diameter of the hole for leading to allow you to mount the workpiece on a tap chuck (figure 6.12J). You may also mount a workpiece bored for leading in an outside-gripping chuck (figure 6.12, K and L), or between centers (figure 6.12, G and H).

Before boring, reduce the lathe speed to that appropriate for the particular drill (*Woodturning Methods*, page 167). To increase the probability that the drill will start boring axially, the end of the workpiece should contain an axial conical, recess to center the drill point. The included angle of this recess should ideally be a little greater than the point angle of the drill. You can hold the workpiece for boring by hand (figure 6.20) or in a chuck (6.21 to 6.23). The latter method tends to result in a more axial hole.

Figure 6.20 Boring a hand-held workpiece. The end being bored was the previously right-hand end when the workpiece, was being roughed as in figure 6.14. I also then trued the right-hand end as in figure 6.16 (and if necessary 6.15) because it was to become the finished bottom of the chessman, and would need to seat nicely against the face of my tap chuck. I used the conical recess left by the tail center to center the drill point.

6.5.5 BORING WITH THE WORKPIECE HELD IN A CHUCK

When you cupchuck a workpiece, the workpiece may not align exactly as it did when it was earlier mounted between centers. If not, you should true the end of the cupchucked workpiece (figure 6.21), and true and enlarge the conical recess left by the drive (or tail) center (figure 6.22) before boring as in figure 6.23.

Figure 6.21 Truing the end with a skew's long point after mounting the workpiece in a chuck. The blank was earlier prepared as shown in figures 6.13 to 6.19.

If you will need to later rechuck the workpiece by the same spigot, make a reference mark on the workpiece which aligns with a feature of the chuck (see figure 6.40).

Figure 6.22 Scraping a central, conical recess into the trued end of the workpiece with a skew's long point. The recess is to center the drill point.

Figure 6.23   Boring the workpiece to the depth signified by the masking tape. This workpiece will be transposed for finish-turning by method *L* in figure 6.12, hence a chucking spigot has been turned on the workpiece's right-hand end as shown in figures 6.17 to 6.19.

6.5.6   UNDERCUTTING

You must chuck the workpiece for boring if you want to undercut the bored hole in the lathe to ensure that the leading cannot slide out. You can also undercut the leading hole by hand later. If you intend to mount the blank on a screwchuck or tap chuck for finish-turning, you do not need to undercut the hole because the thread left by the chuck will retain the leading.

Figure 6.24   Undercutting the left-hand end of the bored hole with the scraper *B* in figure 6.7.

6.6   FINISH-TURNING

Once you have roughed a chessman workpiece, and it is mounted between centers or in a chuck for finish-turning, the first operation is usually to turn the workpiece to a cylinder of diameter equal to the chessman's maximum finished diameter. The resulting cylinder only has to be accurate to diameter in the regions where the chessman's finished diameter equals the maximum. You then continue the finish-turning using the techniques generally used for spindle and, if relevant, cupchuck turning.

When deciding which turning tools and tool techniques you will employ for finish-turning, and the order you will use them in, you are looking for the best compromise between two sometimes-conflicting criteria:

1. *Efficient tool usage.* You will turn more efficiently if you use the roughing gouge, skew chisel, and detail gouge in that order. This principle still applies when the chessman's design requires you to change tool more often, use different sizes of the same tool type, and/or use more types of tool, for example, scrapers and parting tools.
2. *The preservation of workpiece stiffness.* For a spindle turning this means turning the smallest diameters last, and when the workpiece gets slender, finish-turning from the center of the workpiece's length towards the two ends. For a cupchucked workpiece this means working from right to left.

While these criteria apply generally to axially grained workpieces, there are two major differences between the profiles of spindles of typical design and those of chessmen:

1. In chessmen, the beads are often narrower and taller and the coves are deeper and narrower than in typical spindles. Hence you may need tools similar to those shown in figures 6.5 to 6.7.
2. In typical spindles the maximum diameters of the details are usually the same (figure 6.25); in chessmen they often differ. This problem is discussed in figures 6.26 and 6.27, and further illustrated in the sequences showing the finish-turning of chessmen.

There may be further complications, for example the need to interrupt the turning to carve, but I will illustrate typical procedures by describing turning a St. George queen both between centers and with the workpiece cantilevering from a chuck (figures 6.28 to 6.39, and 6.40 to 6.47 respectively).

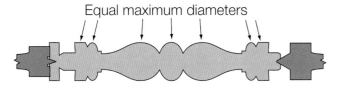

Equal maximum diameters

Figure 6.25   A section through a typical spindle with all its maximum diameters equal.

Figure 6.26   Marking out, V-cutting, and parting when the maximum diameters along a spindle vary.

A parting tool leaves a channel with torn sides and a bottom surface which is little better. Therefore the bottom of a parting-tool cut should not be retained as a finished surface. How therefore can you accurately turn a chessman with beads each having a different maximum diameter? Consider turning the three center beads of a St. George queen. Your options after roughing the workpiece to the maximum finished diameter of the chessman include:

B. Mark the reference points from your pencil gauge. V-cut down to the fillets. Then caliper the bead regions between the pairs of canted V-cuts using a skew or detail gouge with its cutting edge presented with side rake to minimize tear-out.
C. Accurately rough the workpiece to the chessman's unornamented form—this obviates the need to caliper the bead diameters individually. You could use a template of the unornamented form with the reference points marked on its front edge to enable you to accurately turn the form and mark out the details.
D. My preferred method which uses two parting cuts per bead. The method is explained in greater detail in the next figure.

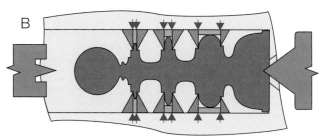

The blank is roughed to a cylinder by removing the yellow wood. The cylinder is marked out from a pencil gauge (purple arrows). Canted V-cuts (red) are made down to the fillets. The bead maximum diameters are then cut with a skew chisel or detail gouge (green). The beads are then rolled, etc.

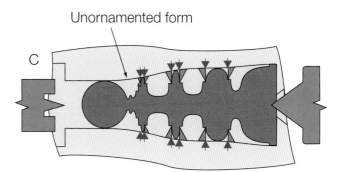

Unornamented form

The blank is roughed to the chessman's unornamented form. The reference points are marked. V-cuts are made down to the fillets (red). The beads are then rolled, etc.

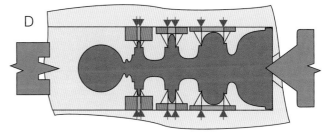

The blank is roughed to a cylinder. The cylinder is marked out from a pencil gauge. The maximum diameters are set with a parting tool alongside the reference points (red). Small V-cuts (not shown here, but see figure 6.27) are made in the corner of each earlier parting cut alongside each bead. These V-cuts transfer the reference points to the smaller diameters. The bead maximum diameters are cut with a skew chisel (green). Canted V-cuts are then taken down to the fillets (yellow). Then the beads are rolled, etc.

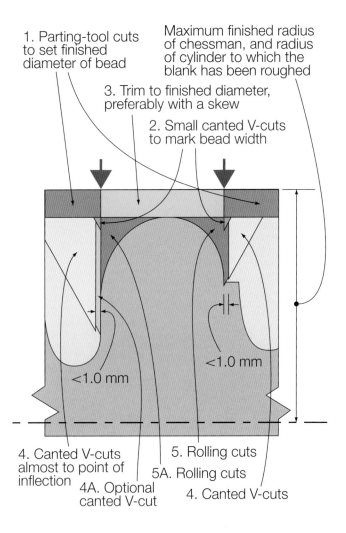

1. Parting-tool cuts to set finished diameter of bead

Maximum finished radius of chessman, and radius of cylinder to which the blank has been roughed

3. Trim to finished diameter, preferably with a skew

2. Small canted V-cuts to mark bead width

<1.0 mm

<1.0 mm

4. Canted V-cuts almost to point of inflection

4A. Optional canted V-cut

5. Rolling cuts

5A. Rolling cuts

4. Canted V-cuts

Figure 6.27   The five steps for turning a bead with a maximum diameter less than the largest finished diameter of the chessman. After pencilling the boundaries of the bead on the cylindrical surface (purple arrows) from the pencil gauge, the five cuts described should be performed in sequence. The steps are also shown in figures 6.29 to 6.32, 6.34, and 6.35.

Cuts *4* can be made with a skew, a parting-off tool, or a parting tool. With the last, the side of the channel nearest the bead should be well away so that no parting-tool tear-out would be left on the surface of the finished bead (figure 6.34).

If you use one rolling cut to produce the whole finished surface of each half of a bead (cuts *5*), you will produce a consistent surface. With very high beads, however, you may find it safer to form the finished side of the bead with one canted V-cut *4A*, and then roll the top with cuts *5A*.

6.6.1   TURNING A CHESSMAN BETWEEN CENTERS

Figures 6.28 to 6.39 show the finish-turning of a St. George queen. This process may be interrupted by operations which could be described as carving, and these are described in the next section 6.7.

Although chessmen turned between centers are spindle turnings, they are rarely slender turnings in the way that, say, stair balusters are. If a chessman is very slender, you may need to use a string steady or a mobile finger steady (*Woodturning Methods*, pages 64 and 65 respectively).

Figure 6.28   Setting the chessman's maximum finished diameter with a roughing gouge and vernier calipers. The rest of the workpiece was then roughed to the same diameter.

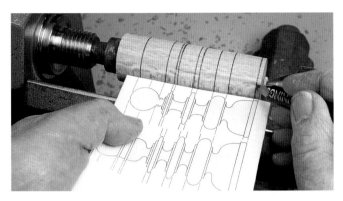

Figure 6.29 Marking the reference points from a paper pencil gauge, folded from a printout of the drawing on page 120.

Figure 6.30 Calipering the diameter of the sphere immediately to the left of its top. The other maximum diameters have been calipered on each side of each bead as explained in figures 6.26D and 6.27.

Figure 6.31 Making the fine V-cuts in the corners of the parting cuts (cuts *2* in figure 6.27).

Figure 6.32 Taking the bands containing maximum diameters down to those maximum diameters (cuts *3* in figure 6.27).

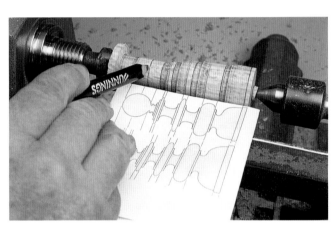

Figure 6.33 Marking the location of the maximum diameter of the sphere. Here I have shaded the waste between the beads.

Figure 6.34 Calipering to the diameters of the fillets.

Figure 6.35   Rolling a bead with a skew's short point.

Figure 6.38   Turning a cove between two fillets.

Figure 6.36   Cutting a fillet with a skew's short point.

Figure 6.39   Turning the neck to the left of the sphere using delicate pointing cuts with a skew's long point. The next operations of sanding and finishing are pictured later in this chapter in figures 6.86 to 6.89.

Figure 6.37   Turning the cove above the base with the gouge pictured on the left in figure 6.6.

6.6.2   TURNING A CUPCHUCKED CHESSMAN WORKPIECE

Figures 6.40 to 6.47 continue from figure 6.19, and show the cupchucked workpiece being finish-turned to the same St. George queen design which was shown being turned between centers in figures 6.28 to 6.39.

Figure 6.40   Roughing the cupchucked workpiece to a cylinder whose diameter equals that of the maximum finished diameter of the queen. Note the pencil mark at the left-hand end of the workpiece which is aligned with the center of chuck jaw number 1. When I later need to rechuck this workpiece, I again align the pencil mark with the center of jaw 1. Together with the precise shoulder, this should ensure that the workpiece will rotate truly.

Figure 6.41   Cutting the end square with a skew's long point. Cuts are taken until the conical impression left by the driving center is eliminated.

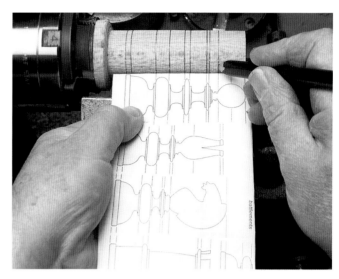

Figure 6.42   Marking out the queen from a folded paper pencil gauge.

Figure 6.43   Planing the length of the sphere to the sphere's maximum diameter. The other three beads have already been planed to their maximum diameters (figure 6.27, cuts *3*) after parting down on each side (figure 6.27, cuts *1*), and marking their boundaries with a skew's long point (figure 6.27, cuts *2*).

Figure 6.44   Rolling the top of the sphere.

Figure 6.47   The queen finish-turned, and ready for sanding and finishing, and then parting-off.

Figure 6.45   Rolling the sphere's left-hand side.

6.7   CARVING AND SPECIAL DETAILS

The details carved in mainly turned sets are usually restricted to

1.   Crosses, usually on the tops of kings.
2.   The points of crowns. Similar details include petals, leaves, and merlons. They are all carved into the walls of turned, cup-shaped forms which imitate or resemble crowns, flower heads, crow's-nests, battlements, etc. These details are particularly associated with Selenus-style men.
3.   Precision, ornamental drilling.
4.   The channels in bishops' miters.
5.   Knights' (horses') heads.
6.   Rooks' battlements.

The techniques associated with carving these details are easier than you may suppose. Practice them on waste wood if you are not confident. However you can almost or completely eliminate the need to carve by designing a set with little or no carving, or by using commercially manufactured piece symbols (figure 6.48).

Figure 6.46   Rolling the left-hand bead.

Figure 6.48   Pieces made using brass piece symbols supplied courtesy of Carba-Tec Ltd.

6.7.1 CARVING CROWNS, FLOWER HEADS, CROW'S-NESTS, ETC.

DESIGN

A crown or similar can be at the top of a chessman, like a finial, or be the base of a chessman. One or more crowns can be positioned along the stem of a chessman (figures 1.37 and 4.10). You may be able to carve and turn such chessmen in one piece, but this may require you to make special tools, especially cranked scrapers, and sanding may be difficult or impossible because of lack of access. To overcome these problems, and also those of slenderness, you can assemble such chessmen from components (figure 6.49).

If your crown is intended to imitate an Eastern crown, it should have twelve points (page 71, figure 3.3). When deciding the number of points for other crowns, be influenced by what is aesthetically appropriate.

MARKING OUT POINTS, PETALS, AND SIMILAR

Points, petals, and longitudinal features such as flutes and reeds, are most conveniently marked onto the workpiece surface using an indexing facility.

Woodturning lathes which have built-in dividing plates typically have 24 (or 48) holes drilled into the outer flange of the largest pulley wheel on the headstock spindle. These holes enable 360° to be divided into 2, 3, 4, 6, 8, 12, and 24 (and 48) equal parts. If you want to divide 360° into any other number of equal parts, or your lathe doesn't have an inbuilt indexing facility, you can readily make a supplementary dividing plate and index (figure 6.2).

You can set out most crown points and similar with your lathe's indexing facility, and by aligning the tool rest at about lathe-axis height close to the wood where you want to mark it (figure 6.79). When the area you need to mark out is strongly curved in diametrical section, use a platform similar to that shown in figure 6.65, and profile an edge of the platform so that it will follow the surface of the workpiece (see also *Woodturning Techniques*, figure 7.99). You can also use this type of platform as a jig for sawing (figures 6.65, 6.68, 6.76 and 6.77), or for cutting with an edge (figure 6.84).

CARVING AND DRILLING

Although ivory, bone, and similar materials are typically substantially harder than wood, they have the advantage that they can be carved without much regard to grain direction. The fibrousness and openness of wood's structure means that

1. Carving against the grain will usually lead to wood splitting away.
2. Carving with the grain can lead to the wood splitting away ahead of the cutting edge.
3. Wood being carved needs to be supported locally. Also, the whole piece of wood being carved must be strong enough and sufficiently supported, or it will rive or shear.

When carving any material, the waste must also be able to escape, if not undesirable crushing may result and the cutting edge is likely to be forced off its intended path. Similarly with drilling, supporting waste is desirable so that the back of a point or petal is not splintered away.

Figures 6.50 to 6.55 show the turning and carving of the chessman pictured in figure 6.49.

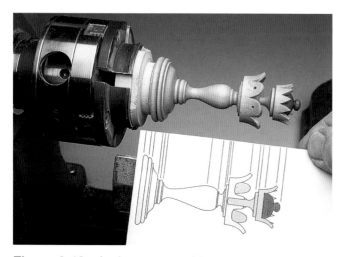

Figure 6.49   A chessman with a crown, and carved and drilled petals. Although the cove to the left of the flower head is large enough in diameter to have been bored to house the stem of the top crown component, I have opted to leave a raised spigot inside the flower head because it is the solution used when all the stems of a chessman are thin.

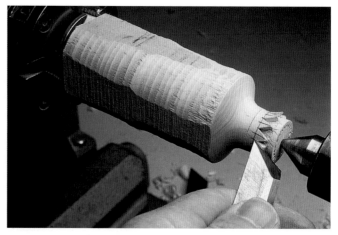

Figure 6.50   Carving the crown's points. After chucking the workpiece, the outside of the crown was finish-turned. A short spigot with a diameter equal to the inside diameter of the tips of the crown points was left to the right of the point tips to provide support to the wood which was then carved away from between the points.

Longitudinal lines along the centers of the points were drawn using the indexing facility, and the left-hand end of the toolrest to guide the pencil, as shown in figure 6.79.

The vees of waste between the points were carved away using about six cuts, three for each edge. The first pair of cuts created a small vee, which was then widened and lengthened using the later cuts. The tailstock provides additional support to the workpiece.

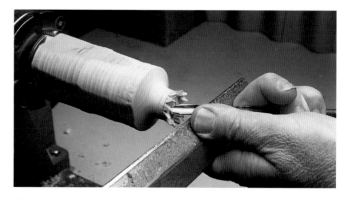

Figure 6.51   Hollowing the crown with a small detail gouge. The scraper *E* in figure 6.7 was then used to flatten the bottom of the hollow in the crown. After finish-turning the rest of the outside of the crown and its supporting stem, the crown component was sanded and parted off.

6.52 Marking out petals using a template cut from a plastic milk container. Longitudinal lines between the petals were first pencilled using the indexing facility and the right-hand end of the toolrest.

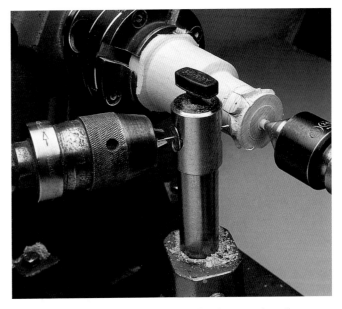

Figure 6.54 Drilling the petals, here using the Robert Sorby Precision Boring System with a homemade bush. A simple, homemade, wood drilling jig is shown in *Woodturning Methods*, page 180. Next, the inside of the flower head will be hollowed as described in figure 6.51, taking care to leave the upstanding spigot.

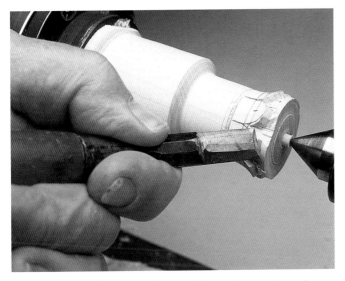

Figure 6.53 Carving the petals using a bevel-edged chisel, *C* in figure 6.8. I could have used chisels with the skewed edges (figure 6.50). Equally, I could have used the chisel shown in this figure to carve the crown points. I could also have made preliminary saw cuts between the points or petals.

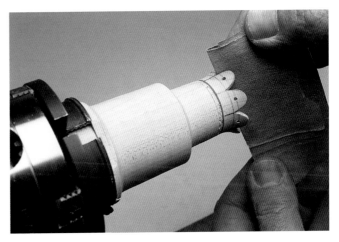

Figure 6.55 Sanding between the petals. The rest of this lower component is then bored, finish-turned, sanded, and the crown component and the crown's cap glued in to reach the stage shown in figure 6.49.

6.7.2 CARVING CROSSES

Four types of cross were introduced in figure 3.9. You produce crosses by turning their edges and carving their faces. Figures 6.56 to 6.64 show turning and carving a cross patée on top of a St. George king.

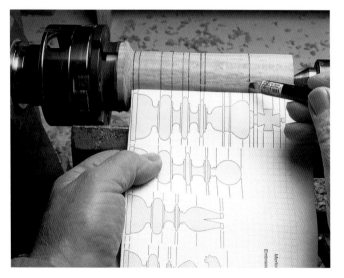

Figure 6.56 Marking the reference lines onto the rotating workpiece from a paper pencil gauge. The workpiece has been roughed to the king's maximum finished diameter.

Figure 6.57 Making a canted V-cut of type *2* shown in figure 6.27. The outside diameter of the cross has been calipered at both ends of the cross.

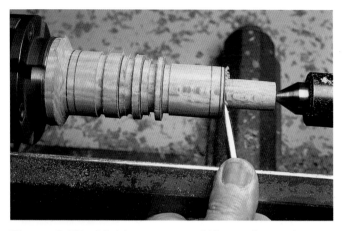

Figure 6.58 Making a canted V-cut down the top of the crown. The top of the crown needs to be finish-turned to allow access to turn the left-hand end of the cross.

The right-hand end of the workpiece has been turned down to the maximum finished diameter of the cross.

Figure 6.59 Marking out the cross.

Figure 6.60 I have parted down to the diameter at the tips of cross's top and bottom arms. Because there was insufficient room to the left of the bottom arm, I have parted down over that arm.

Figure 6.61 Starting to cut the top of the cross's left and right arms with a skew's long point.

Figure 6.62 Cutting the cross's bottom arm with a narrow skew's short point. The central cylindrical section of the cross should be sanded before carving the cross faces.

Figure 6.63 Using a skewed, bevel-edged chisel to cut away part of the turned cross to leave a flat face. A square ended bench chisel can also be used.

Figure 6.64 The cross completed. The rest of the king will then be finish-turned, working from right to left.

6.7.3 CUTTING MITER CHANNELS

Most chess miters have a deep channel, usually of rectangular or trapezoidal cross section, cut through the miter's turned form. The channel can be vertical, helical, or canted as in the Staunton bishop.

  If you intend to cut the channels by hand, either by sawing followed by carving (figures 6.65 to 6.67), or by sawing alone (figure 6.68), they are better cut before the miters' outer shapes are turned, but can be cut after. Power sawn channels should be cut before the bishops are finish-turned (figure 6.69).

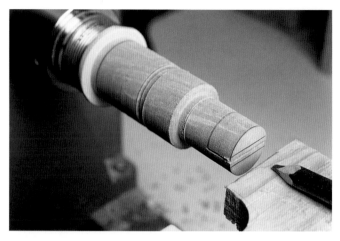

Figure 6.66   Marking the end edges of a near-triangular, trapezoidal sectioned channel. By raising the sawing platform, I was able to mark a first horizontal line on the end of the workpiece. I then indexed the workpiece 180°, and marked the second horizontal line.

Figure 6.65   Hand sawing a diametrical cut using a sawing platform. The workpiece is held on a screwchuck, and has been roughed to the bishop's maximum finished diameter, and marked out. The miter section has been turned to its finished, maximum diameter.

  The spigot of the sawing platform's stem fits snugly into the banjo. The shoulder on the stem rests on the top of the banjo, and locates the top of the platform so that a rip saw resting on it saws exactly at lathe-axis height. The annular piece of cardboard was glued to the stem's shoulder to correct the platform's height. I have waxed the top of the platform so that the saw will slide freely.

Figure 6.67   The miter in the preceding figure after carving away the channel waste using the skewed bevel-edged chisels shown, and finish-turning.

Figure 6.68 Hand sawing the sloping sides of a miter channel, thus avoiding the need to carve them. The height of the sloping-topped sawing platform and the distance of its left-hand edge from the end of the miter must be the same for all four bishops of a set if their channels are to have the same cross section.

Figure 6.69 Power sawing a miter's channel. These workpieces will be mounted on a tap chuck for finish-turning.

The channels of some mass-produced miters have bottoms which have the shape of a shallow inverted vee. Such channels can be cut by pushing the workpiece only part way over a circular saw blade, the distance being regulated by a stop. For this the workpiece can be held vertically as here, horizontally, or at any angle in between.

6.7.4 CARVING HORSES' HEADS

A horse's head can be carved separately, and later pinned or screwed to its base; or the head can be carved and the base turned into the one piece of wood. There is little to choose between the two methods, and the pre-carving steps for both are shown in figures 6.70 to 6.72. The carving and finish-turning of a one-piece knight are shown in figures 6.73 and 6.74.

Figure 6.75 shows a traditional method for turning large numbers of horse's head carving blanks.

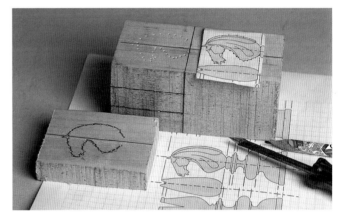

Figure 6.70 Marking out. *Left,* a horse's head blank. *Back,* a one-piece knight. I have transferred the outlines of the horse's head by pricking through the paper, and drawing through the resulting holes. You could also use carbon paper, or glue an elevation of the horse's head onto the workpiece.

Figure 6.71 Preliminary turning. *Top,* a pin, which will later be glued into a hole bored into the turned base, has been turned on the head. *Bottom,* a chucking spigot has been turned on the workpiece.

Figure 6.72   Bandsawing the horses' heads. The workpiece on the right is about to have the waste horse heads sawn away—these could be bored, carved, and mounted on bases turned with a spigot.

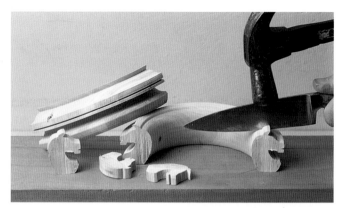

Figure 6.75   A profiled ring being rived into horse's head blanks, ready for carving. The technique is described in *Woodturning Techniques*, pages 93 to 97.

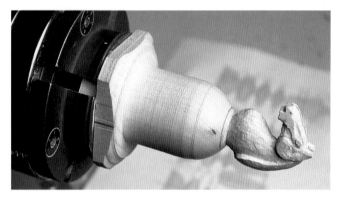

Figure 6.73   The head roughly carved. Before carving a horse's head and neck ensure that you thoroughly know the details of the form you want to carve.

6.7.5   CARVING ROOKS' BATTLEMENTS

DESIGN
There are usually, but do not have to be, an even number of embrasures and merlons in a rook's battlement. (If you have an odd number, the embrasures have to be cut by hand). Six embrasures are often the most aesthetically pleasing, but four better represent the four directions at right angles in which a rook can move. You must also decide whether the tops of the crenels and the bottoms of the embrasures will be horizontal or slope downwards and outwards as in figure 3.32. Other variables include the depth of the embrasures, the depth of the alur (which is usually greater than that of the embrasures), and the shape of the battlement in diametrical section. A minor variable is whether the two vertical edges of each merlon lie along radiuses from the rook's axis (figure 6.76), or are parallel to one another (figure 6.77).

CARVING AWAY EMBRASURES
Embrasures can be cut by hand (figures 6.76 to 6.78). They can also be cut with a table saw or similar (figures 6.79 to 6.80).

Alurs are best hollowed after the embrasures are cut (figures 6.81 and 6.82).

Figure 6.74   The knight carved, finish-turned, and sanded.

CARVING THE JOINTS BETWEEN ASHLARS
An ashlar is a square-cut building stone (it can also be
a stone facing). Figures 6.83 and 6.84 show how to
imitate the horizontal and vertical joints between
ashlars.

Figure 6.76   Sawing merlons with radial edges.
Because there were an even number of embrasures
and their bottoms were to be horizontal, I could
make diametrical saw cuts. The radial spacing of the
cuts was achieved using the indexing facility.

The workpiece is held on a tap chuck, has been
turned to a cylinder whose diameter equals the
maximum finished diameter of the rook, and has
been marked out from a paper pencil gauge.

Figure 6.77   Sawing merlons with parallel edges.
This was achieved by raising the sawing platform
top by an appropriate distance above lathe-axis
height.

**Figure 6.78   Paring away the waste between the
saw cuts to create the embrasures** with the
narrow square-ended chisel shown in figure 6.83.
How to power saw embrasures is shown in the next
two figures.

**Figure 6.79   Marking reference lines for power
sawing the embrasures.** Because there will be six
embrasures, with a 24-hole dividing plate I need just
three lines indexed at four-hole intervals.

6.80   Power sawing embrasures. Take care, because although this jig prevents you having to hand-hold the workpiece, the blade guard needs to be lifted.

A single diametrical cut leaves an embrasure equal in width to the saw kerf. To widen the embrasures, cut with each reference line on the workpiece aligned with the 1 mark on the jig; widening cuts are then taken with each reference line aligned with the 2 mark.

If you want the bottoms of the embrasures to slope, push the rook only part way over the exposed blade against a stop.

Prefer a saw blade which leaves a flat-bottomed kerf.

Figure 6.81   Using a small detail gouge to hollow the alur and shape the inside surfaces of the merlons.

Figure 6.82   Deepening and flattening the bottom of the alur with scraper *E* in figure 6.7.

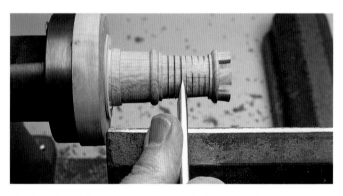

6.83   V-cutting with a skew's long point to imitate the horizontal joints between the ashlars.

Figure 6.84   Pushing in the cutting edge of a square-ended chisel to imitate vertical joints between ashlars. The chisel is guided by the sawing platform shown earlier in figures 6.76 and 6.77. The workpiece is appropriately indexed between cutting each longitudinal row of joints. The vertical joints in adjacent rows are usually staggered by half the width of an ashlar.

6.8 ORNAMENTING AND TEXTURING

Turned chessmen are usually ornamented with turned moldings and conventional carving, but despite their small sizes and absences of large plane areas, there are many other "turning" techniques which can be applied

1. Ornamental turning, a technique which has been applied surprisingly infrequently (figure 6.85). An allied technique is rose-engine turning.
2. Eccentric turning including therming.
3. Multi-axis turning.
4. Elliptical turning.
5. Ornamental and precision drilling

6. Surface texturing. You can texture by hand away from the lathe using conventional carving tools or punches. You can also texture a workpiece as it rotates in the lathe using a chatter tool, coarse abrasive paper or cloth, a wire brush (either being rotated by a separate power source or not), or a knurling-type tool (for example, the Robert Sorby Spiralling System). There are many texts which describe texturing.[4]

6.9 SANDING

After finish-turning, some sand and then polish almost unthinkingly. Similarly among buyers there is an unthinking expectation that wood should be offered sanded and polished. If your turning techniques are good, there is no necessity to sand. Similarly whether the men are sanded or not, there is no necessity to polish. You should consciously decide at the design stage whether you will sand, and/or polish, how, and to what standards.

Figure 6.85   Ornamentally-turned African blackwood rooks by Jon Sauer of Pacifica, California.

Figure 6.86   Sanding the queen shown in figure 6.39. Note the rack for abrasive papers.[3]

How to sand spindles is described on pages 117 and 125 of *The Fundamentals of Woodturning*. Typically you start sanding chessmen with an abrasive grit size between 150 and 220. Use A-weight, aluminum oxide, opencoat, abrasive paper rather than abrasive cloth because paper folds to a sharper edge. For the final sanding operation I use 400 grit size, but many will go finer; I also prefer silicon carbide paper because its grit is sharper than aluminum oxide grit. If there is a choice, do not to sand areas which have to be carved until after the carving is completed to avoid unnecessarily blunting your carving tools.

If a chessman's bottom is to be baized, you should not need to sand it. If the bottom will not be baized, it should preferably be sanded. Sand off any sharpness left on the outer edge of the bottom so that the man will be less likely to damage the chess board, and the other men of the set if they are not stored separated.

6.10   DECORATING AND FINISHING

There are an increasing number of books, magazine articles, etc. which illustrate the unlimited decorating and finishing possibilities.[4] I am not an expert on either, and will restrict my advice to clear (translucent) finishing.

"CLEAR" FINISHING
Chessmen are often stained to create a side signature. Wood is best stained before polishing (clear finishing)—putting stain into the polish deadens the wood's appearance.

There is no clear finish or finishing method which is demonstrably far superior to others. The variables which you should consider when specifying the finishing materials and their methods of application include:

1. Your desired gloss level. You can vary the gloss level of a surface by how finely you abrade it before or after finishing, and by burnishing it. You can also vary the gloss level of a surface by selecting a particular finishing compound (some are available in several gloss levels), by how you apply it, and by selecting a particular thinning compound and the

proportion you use.
2. The apparent final thickness of the surface layer of polish.
3. The translucency of the finish.
4. Whether the polish can have any tint (most are pale brown, and will therefore tint the wood). If you desire to use an untinted polish you can use two-part polyurethane or an untinted nitrocellulose lacquer, both of which give off undesirable vapors. Among the much-less-toxic alternatives are water-based polyurethane, and white shellac.
5. The required durability of the finished surface. How resistant should it be to handling, abrasion, and water and other solvents?
6. The ease and method of removal and repair. Finishes change over time, mainly due to attack by ultraviolet radiation; they also suffer mechanical damage and gradual wear.
7. Do you want to encourage the formation of a patina from handling?
8. The toxicity of the finishing materials, and your exposure to them. The efficiency of any fume and dust extraction you may have. The dust from sanding finishes can also be a health hazard.
9. The finishing facilities you have; for example, how dust free your polishing area can be.

Turners have the advantage over other woodworkers when finishing of being able to rotate a workpiece both when applying a finish and when sanding between other finishing operations. You should not therefore remove waste wood which is necessary to hold a chessmen in the lathe until you have to. This may mean you have to separately finish small end areas, but this disadvantage does not outweigh the main gain.

You may choose to perform the first finishing operation on each man immediately after turning and sanding it. Alternatively, and usually preferably, finish the men in batches, which will usually require them to be rechucked in the lathe at least once.

Below I describe the finishing method I use for chessmen

1. If the decorative intention will not be destroyed by a slight brown tint, apply Danish oil or gloss one-part polyurethane varnish thinned about 10% with

turpentine substitute (white or mineral spirit). Yes, you are supposed to use lacquer thinner, but turps seems fine in this low proportion. Slop the polish on with a brush until absorption ceases, either with the workpiece rotating slowly or the lathe switched off (figure 6.87).

2. With the lathe running slowly, wipe off the surplus polish with paper towels or white, lint-free cloth (figure 6.88). (Cloth can get caught by the rotating parts and pull you in, paper towels are therefore safer because they tear readily). Don't press too hard because you want to leave a slight film on the surface. Do not use strongly colored paper towels or cloths because the dyes are absorbed from them by the polish, and then transferred to the workpiece, usually as highly-visible streaks.

3. Once the polish has set fully (I usually leave it overnight), I sand with 400 silicon carbide paper. If the grain has not been raised perceptibly, don't sand.

4. Streaks and blotchiness rarely occur with the first coat of polish, but are likely when hand applying second and later coats. Instead of applying a second coat of polish, therefore apply one of the woodturners shellac/wax-based instant polishes such as Shellawax (figure 6.89). (I find that they sink-in if applied to raw wood, but give a long-lasting sheen if applied over sealed wood). Follow the manufacturers instructions, which generally advise applying the compound to stationary or slowly-rotating wood, followed by pressing with cloth or a paper towel onto the fast-rotating wood.

Figure 6.87 Brushing on the clear finish, here Danish oil, with the lathe running very slowly.

Figure 6.88 Wiping off the surplus Danish oil after applying more than needed and allowing it to soak in. After it has fully set, I lightly sand with 400 grit silicon carbide abrasive paper.

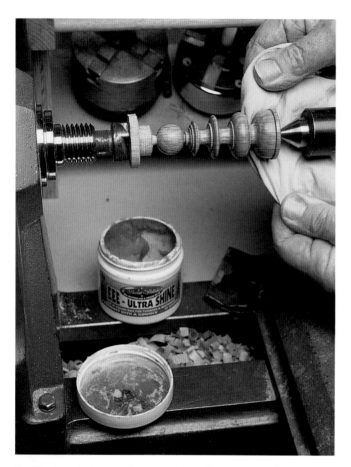

6.89 Friction-polishing after the second sanding. The man is then parted off, the top of the sphere trimmed and sanded, and that area patch polished.

Figure 6.90 Tools for parting-off.
Left, a skew with about a 20° sharpening angle which enables a chessman to be parted-off closer to the chuck. Its right-hand bevel is at about 5° to its right-hand face; its left-hand bevel is at about 15° to its left-hand face.

6.11 PARTING-OFF

Parting is cutting a narrow rectangular channel which does not reach the lathe axis, and which usually has its bottom diameter calipered. Parting-off or -through is similar except that the workpiece is severed. With a chessman, the need to sever the finish-turned (and usually finished) man from its chucking spigot is associated with the need to leave the man's bottom flat or slightly concave, and smooth.

Although you can part off with a parting tool or a skew chisel, the two tools designed for parting-off, and shown in figures 6.90 and 6.91, enable you to part-off closer to a chuck, and leave the turning's left-hand end smoother than a parting tool can.

6.91 Parting-off with a parting-off skew chisel. Whichever tool you use, do not rush the cuts. Keep sufficient clearance to the left so that the tool is not forced to the right against the bottom of the chessman. The widening waste cuts should leapfrog ahead of the finishing cuts until close to severance.

6.12 LEADING

Lead is more commonly used for leading (or loading) chessmen than the other suitable materials specified in Table 6.1 because it is unusually dense, relatively cheap, widely available in different forms (sheet, shot, washers, etc.), has a relatively low melting point, and has a high surface tension when molten which aids accurate pouring.

You can fill the hole bored into the bottom of a chessman by

1. Pouring in molten lead (figure 6.92).
2. Gluing in a cast cylinder of lead (figure 6.92).
3. Pushing in a mortar of small lead pieces or lead shot (obtainable from gun shops) in epoxy.
4. Gluing or screwing in pieces of other metals.

If you intend to lead by pouring molten lead into the men and if the holes' walls are not threaded, undercut the bored holes to ensure that the plugs of lead will not drop out. You can undercut in the lathe with a scraper after boring a chuck-held workpiece (figure 6.24), or you can widen the bottom of the hole by hand away from the lathe with a narrow chisel or gouge. An alternative to undercutting is to partially drive a woodscrew axially into the bottom of the bored hole.

6.92 Leading chessmen. *Right front*, a split mold held together with C clamps for casting cylinders of lead which can be glued into the bored holes into chessman. *Right rear*, pouring molten lead into inverted chessmen.

I melted the lead in a small, cast-iron pan on a domestic gas ring—an electric hob is also suitable. The pan should have a lip or spout to aid precise pouring. I used plumbers sheet lead cut into small pieces about 1 to 1.5 in. (25 to 40 mm) square. The lead may take several minutes to melt, and then hides under a thin film of lead oxide. Between meltings, I throw the lead oxide residue away.

The men should be securely positioned vertical and upside down in a rack, frame, or similar. Do not hand-hold the men when you pour in the lead, you may get badly burnt. Do not pour molten lead into a chessman unless the wood is fully seasoned. If you do, the phreatic steam formed will cause a fountain of molten lead to erupt from the cavity. Even if the wood is seasoned, the steam generated during leading can affect the polished surface "downgrain" from the lead.

The lead will shrink as it cools. Therefore fill to about 1/4 in. (6 mm) from the top of the hole, allow the lead to partially cool and any minor bubbling to occur, and then top up. If the lead protrudes, cut it back with a carving gouge or chisel. You may also fill the hole flush with epoxy. The bottom of a neatly leaded chessman is not unsightly, but is often baized.

Table 6.1 The specific gravities of wood and of materials which can be used for leading		
Material	*Specific gravity (density) in grams per cc.*	*Melting point ° C*
Seasoned wood	0.2 – 1.1	n.a.
Tin	7.3	232
Iron	7.0 – 7.9	n.a.
Steel	7.6 – 7.8	n.a.
Brass	8.2 – 8.6	n.a.
Lead	11.3	327
Tungsten	19.3	n.a.
Platinum	21.4	n.a.

Solder is a combination of tin and lead and its properties lie between those of the two metals

6.13   BAIZING

Chessmen slide pleasingly on a horizontal chess board if their bottoms are smooth and turned flat or very slightly concave, but not convex. The bottoms of chessmen are baized to slide even more freely, and, if the men are leaded, to cover the plug of lead. I use the term *baized* because baize or thin leather are preferred to felt, which is a rather loose fabric. I buy baize offcuts from a manufacturer of snooker and pool tables.

You can cut disks of leather or baize with wad punches (figure 6.93), or in your lathe (figures 6.94). You then glue the disks onto the bottoms of the men, usually with PVA glue.

6.94   Cutting baize disks in the lathe. The disk of wood on the screwchuck has a flat, true, right-hand face. The sizing disk located by the tail center has been turned to the required diameter of the baize disks, and also has a concave left-hand face so that the roughly cut pieces of baize are gripped tightly close to where they will be cut. I present the detail gouge so that its bevel is supported by the periphery of the sizing disk, before cutting the baize. The lathe speed is not critical, but I use about 1000 rpm. I cut up to eight baize disks at a time.

6.14   ENDNOTES

1. Gareth Williams "How Games are Made" *The Chess Collector* (July 1997): p.13.

2. A set with one side turned and carved from transparent amber and the other side from cloudy amber is pictured in Charles K. Wilkinson and Jessie McNab Dennis. *Chess: East & West, Past & Present* (New York: Metropolitan Museum of Art, 1968), set 100.

3. Mike Darlow "A Turner's Sandpaper Rack" *Woodwork* (April 2004): pp. 70–71.

4. One of the best manuals on decorating turnings is Liz & Michael O'Donnell, *Decorating Turned Wood* (Lewes, East Sussex: Guild of Master Craftsman Publications, 2002). Another source is *Woodturning* (April 2004): pp. 15 to 21.

6.93   Cutting baize with a wad punch. I prefer the in-lathe method shown in the next figure which is little slower, avoids the need to buy expensive wad punches, and allows you to cut disks of any diameter.

Chapter Seven

WHERE NEXT?

The properties of wood have caused many useful objects once commonly made in wood to be now only manufactured in plastic, metal, or ceramic materials. Wooden chessmen have not been rendered technically obsolete by these synthetic materials and modern manufacturing methods, although they allow chessmen to be made more cheaply. Also, many players continue to prefer wooden chessmen because of wood's particular tactile properties.

As the bibliography which follows shows, chessmen have their own small, but distinguished, literature. That literature focuses on carved sets, and has been written by scholars and collectors, rarely by makers. This book concentrates on turned chessmen, and is written by a maker, albeit one who has not made many chess sets; it is also my first substantial contribution to the woodturning-projects genre (as opposed to technique, design, and philosophy). Encouragingly, the reactions from those I have contacted in connection with writing this book have been very positive. I am optimistic, therefore, that *Turned Chessmen* will enthuse woodworkers and woodturners to produce chess sets for themselves, as gifts, and to sell; and that this will give pleasure both to those sets' makers and future owners. I hope also that chess-set collectors and chess players will find this book a rewarding read and a useful reference.

I discussed this book's genesis in its introduction, and stated that the related subjects of checkers (draughts), and boxes, boards and tables for checkers and chess, would be the subject of my next woodturning projects book. To stimulate your interest, I present some pictures in figures 7.1 to 7.3. And "yes", I intend to write woodturning projects books on other types of treen.

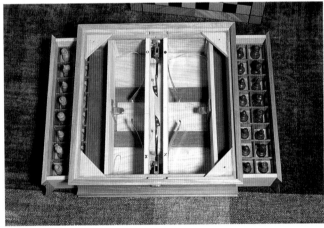

Figure 7.1   A chess set and box by Andrew Lake of New Berrima, Australia. Each drawer springs open when its button on the side of the box is pressed.

Figure 7.3   A chess table and chairs made by Michael Cullen of Petaluma, California.

Figure 7.3   A seventeenth-century combined chess and backgammon board in the Lobkowicz Collections at Nelahozeves Castle in the Czech Republic (also the source of these photographs).

BIBLIOGRAPHIES

Samuel Johnson put it well: "When we inquire into any subject, the first thing we have to do is to know what books have treated of it". Thousands of books have been published on chess, most about playing it or about particular games. Fortunately a more manageable number of books in English have been published on chessmen and on the history of chess, and most are listed below.

Those interested in chessmen are fortunate in being able to subscribe to *The Chess Collector*. A continuing source of detailed information, and of the latest research and discoveries, it is the quarterly journal of the Chess Collectors International. For membership contact: Mr Gareth Williams, "The Gate House", Pencraig, Ross-on-Wye, Herefordshire HR9 6HR, England.

BOOKS ON CHESSMEN

These books also usually provide brief histories of chess.

Allan, James, ed. *Islamic Art in the Ashmolean-Part 1*. Vol 10, *Oxford Studies in Islamic Art*, 1995. The last section of 43 pages is devoted to Islamic ivory chessmen, checkers, and dice.

Finkel, Irving. *The Lewis Chessmen and What Happened to Them*. London: British Museum Press, 1995.

Greygoose, Frank. *Chessmen*. Sydney, Australia: A. H. & A. W. Reed, 1979.

Hammond, Alex. *The Book of Chessmen*. London: Arthur Barker, 1950.

Harbeson, John F. *Nine Centuries of Chessmen, The Collection of John F. Harbeson*. Philadelphia: Philadelphia Museum of Art, 1964.

Katz, Emile. *History of Chessmen*. London: 1963.

Keats, Victor. *Chessmen for Collectors*. London: B. T. Batsford, 1985. This has also been published as *The Illustrated Guide to World Chess Sets*.

Graham, F. Lanier. *Chess Sets*. London: Studio Vista, 1968.

Knight, Bryan M. *The Chess Nut's Fascinating History of Chess Pieces and Internationally Recognized Laws of Chess*. Montreal, Canada: Chess Nut Books, 1973.

Liddell, Donald M. *Chessmen*. London: George G. Harrap, 1938.

Linder, I. M. *The Art of Chess Pieces*. Moscow: H.G.S. Publishers, 1994.

Loranth, Alice N. *Enchanted Chessmen: A World of Fantasy*. Ohio: Cleveland Public Library, John G. White Collection of Chess, 1996.

Mackett-Beeson, A. E. J. *Chessmen*. London: Octopus Books, 1973.

Mark, Michael. *Antique Indian Chess Sets*. Germany: Forderkreis Schach-Geschichtsforschung e.V., 1998.

Mark, Michael. *British Chess Sets*, 2nd ed. London: 1996.

Mayer, Steve. *Bishop Verses Knight: The Verdict*. London: B. T. Batsford, 1997.

Munger, Ned. *Cultures Chess & Art*, four volumes. Box 2543, San Anselmo, CA 94979, USA: Mundial Press, 1996-.

Pennell, Mike. *Chessmen and Intellectual Property*. Venice: 1993.

Schafroth, Colleen. *The Art of Chess*. New York: Harry N. Abrams, 2002.

Stratford, Neil. *The Lewis Chessmen*. London: British Museum Press, 1997.

Taylor, Michael. *The Lewis Chessmen*. London: British Museum Publications, 1978.

The Art of Chess. Edited by Catherine Phillips. London: Gilbert Collection Trust, 2003. Catalogue of the exhibition "The Art of Chess" held at Somerset House, London, from 28th June to 28th September, 2003.

Turnbull, William Peveril. *Chessmen in Action*. London: Routledge, 1914.

Wichmann, Hans and Siegfried. *Chess: The Story of Chesspieces from Antiquity to Modern Times*. London: Paul Hamlyn, 1964.

Wilkinson, Charles K. and Dennis, Jessie M. *Chess: East & West, Past & Present*. New York: Metropolitan Museum of Art, 1968.

Williams, Gareth. *Master Pieces*. Sydney: Allen & Unwin, 2000.

Williams, Gareth. *The Amazing Book of Chess*. London: Tiger Books, 1995.

Yalom, Marilyn. *Birth of the Chess Queen*. London: Rivers Oram, 2004.

BOOKS ON THE HISTORY OF CHESS

Books on chess history usually contain information and illustrations concerning chessmen and chess equipment.

Allen, George. *The Life of Philidor*. Philadelphia: Butter, 1863. Reprint, New York: Da Capo Press, 1971.

Cardo, Horatio. *The Story of Chess*. New York: Abbeville Press, 1998.

Chandler, Murray and Keene, Ray. *The English Chess Explosion*. London: B. T. Batsford.

Davidson, Henry A. *A Short History of Chess*. New York: Geenberg, 1949.

Eales, Richard. *Chess: the History of a Game*. London: B. T. Batsford, 1985.

Falkener, E. *Games Ancient and Oriental and How to Play Them*. London: 1892.

Finkenzeller, Roswin; Ziehr, Wilhelm; and Bührer, Emil M. *Chess: A Celebration of 200 Years*. London: Macenzie Publishing, 1990.

Golombek, Harry. *Chess A History*. New York: G. P. Putnam's Sons, 1976.

Gizycki, Jerzy. *A History of Chess*. London: The Abbey Library, 1972.

Hooper, David and Whyld, Kenneth. *The Oxford Companion to Chess*. Oxford University Press, 1984.

Keats, Victor. *The Illustrated Guide to World Chess Sets*. New York: St. Martin's Press, 1985.

Keats, Victor. *Chess Its Origin*. A translation with commentary of Thomas Hyde's *De Ludibus Orientalibus* (Oxford, 1694). Vol. 2, Oxford Academia Publishers, 1994.

Keene, Raymond. *Chess An Illustrated History*. New York: Simon and Schuster, 1990.

Levitt, Gerald M. *The Turk, Chess Automaton*. Jefferson, North Carolina, McFarland & Co., 2000.

Murray, Harold J. R. *A History of Chess*. Oxford University Press, 1913.

Parlett, David. *The Oxford History of Board Games*. Oxford University Press, 1999.

Whyld, Ken. *Café de la Régence*. Caistor, Lincolnshire: 1953.

Wilson, Fred. *A Pictorial History of Chess*. New York: Dover Publications, 1981.

INDEX